D1481828

# The
# life of the
# Buddha

Patricia M. Herbert

THE BRITISH LIBRARY

*Namo tassa bhagavato arahato samma sambuddhassa*

*Homage to Him, the Blessed, the Worthy, the Fully Enlightened*

# *Preface*

The purpose of this book is to introduce readers in the English-speaking world to the life and teachings of the Buddha as narrated and depicted in Burmese manuscript sources. To do so, openings selected from two of the British Library's finest Burmese life of the Buddha manuscripts are illustrated in 30 double-page colour spreads accompanied by a simple narrative text running beneath the pictures. This presentation retains the format and spirit of the original manuscripts, reproducing them in virtual facsimile, but a little reduced in size and with an English text in place of the Burmese. In these pages the reader encounters vibrant scenes of palace, monastic and everyday life that glow with colour and rich gilding, and enters a world where the old gods and spirits as well as men pay homage to the Buddha and his teaching. The story of one of the world's truly great religious and moral teachers is simply told, and is enhanced by the little-known but glorious manuscript art of Burma.

Some background information on Buddhism and Buddhist art in general is provided in the Introduction, together with rather more detail on Burmese manuscript art. The Appendix (p. 81-95) contains notes on the Buddhist context to help readers who may be unfamiliar with Buddhist terms and concepts and also notes on the art of each page illustrated so that this book may also serve as a reference source for art historians. For although there is no shortage of scholarly and popular books on Buddhism, nor of glossy books reproducing masterpieces of Buddhist art, the art and traditions of Burma in particular have received rather less attention.

Throughout the book, the Pali form of names and terms is used for consistency although the Sanskrit form is occasionally also cited when it is deemed more familiar, and some Burmese versions of the original Pali are also provided. Diacritics appear only in the glossary of names (p. 94-95).

I wish especially to thank my esteemed Buddhist colleague and friend, K. D. Somadasa, for his encouragement and advice to me in the course of writing this book; also John Okell, Noel Singer and U Thaw Kaung. Thanks are also due to Terry Barringer, Librarian of the Royal Commonwealth Society and to the staff of the Oriental and India Office Collections' photographic service. Finally, this book is dedicated to my daughter Juliette, but I also hope – in the manner of all Buddhist dedicatory statements – that much merit may accrue to the British Library by the virtuous deed of publishing this life of the revered Buddha.

Patricia M. Herbert

LONDON, AUGUST 1992

*Left*  The Buddha's first sermon.
Or. 14297, f. 26, detail.

3

# Introduction

Buddhism, one of the great religions of the world, owes its origin to the inspiration of one man who became known as the Buddha, meaning 'The Enlightened One'. The Buddha lived and preached in India over 2,500 years ago, although his exact dates are still a subject for scholarly debate. In some Buddhist countries 544/543 BC traditionally marks the date of the Buddha's death and the beginning of the Buddhist Era, and it is in accordance with this date that the first 2,500 years of the Buddhist faith were celebrated in 1956-57. The Buddha is also known by the title Sakyamuni (meaning sage of the Sakya people) and by the name Gotama (in Sanskrit, Gautama), which is used throughout the Pali Buddhist canon and distinguishes him from other (non-historical) Buddhas believed to have preceded him. His followers addressed him as Bhagava ('lord' or 'blessed one') while he usually referred to himself as Tathagatha – an enigmatic epithet meaning 'thus come' or 'thus gone' and sometimes rendered as 'he who has discovered the truth'. His name as a young man was Siddhattha (in Sanskrit, Siddhartha, meaning 'aim accomplished'), and until he achieved Supreme Enlightenment he is referred to as a Bodhisatta (in Sanskrit, Bodhisattva) – that is, a being who is dedicated to achieving Enlightenment, a 'future Buddha'.

The basic details of the Buddha's life are as follows. He was the son of a chief of the Sakyas, a small tribe of the Himalayan foothills, and was born at Kapilavatthu in what is now southern Nepal. Renouncing the privileged and luxurious life of his father's court, he became at the age of 29 a wandering religious mendicant and embarked on a search for the true meaning of life. Only after abandoning extreme ascetic practices and as a result of profound meditation, did he achieve Enlightenment, and realize a state of blissful mental calm known as *Nibbana* (in Sanskrit, *Nirvana*). The Buddha conceived a new doctrine capable of putting an end to suffering and achieving complete peace. His teachings (the *Dhamma*) attracted many disciples who formed a community or Buddhist order of monks (the *Sangha*). After many years of ministry, the Buddha died at the age of 80, attaining *Parinibbana*, or total escape from the cycle of rebirth and death. His remains were cremated and his relics were placed in commemorative monuments known as stupas.

In time Buddhist Councils were held and the Buddha's teachings gathered together and arranged as scriptures, known as the *Tipitaka* ('Three Baskets') of which the first section, the Vinayapitaka ('Basket of Discipline'), deals with the organization and discipline of monks; the second, the *Suttapitaka* ('Basket of Discourses'), gives the Buddha's teachings and sermons; and the third, the *Abhidhammapitaka* ('Basket of Ultimate Doctrine'), offers a complex systematization of the whole. It was the monks who preserved the Buddha's teachings, at first by committing them to memory and then by recording and copying the Buddhist canon and producing commentaries and other Buddhist texts. Many monasteries became great centres of learning, attracting students from distant countries and organizing Buddhist missions. As a result, Buddhism spread in the course of several centuries south from India to Sri Lanka and Burma, Thailand, Laos and

*Left* The Buddha, sheltered by the Mucalinda Naga.
Or. 14297, f. 23, detail.

Cambodia, and north to Central Asia, Tibet, China, Vietnam, Korea and Japan. The school of Buddhism that spread northwards became known as Mahayana (the Great Vehicle) Buddhism and developed many different forms (among them, Tantric and Zen Buddhism) and the school that spread southwards became known as Theravada (the Way of the Elders) Buddhism or Hinayana (the Lesser Vehicle) Buddhism – a term not favoured by Theravada Buddhists. Theravada Buddhism is also sometimes referred to as Pali Buddhism, Pali being the name of the ancient language in which its canonical texts are preserved. In India, the land of the Buddha's birth, Buddhism was in time eclipsed by Hinduism and by the advent of Islam. Although Buddhism was encountered and studied by many Western missionaries, travellers and colonial administrators, it was only in the 20th century that different forms of Buddhism were introduced to Western countries and Buddhist monasteries and communities established there.

The *Tipitaka* (in Sanskrit, *Tripitaka*) texts are most extensive and very complex and contain much information on the Buddha's life and ministry. But, since the scriptures are arranged by subject and form or length, this information is scattered and not in any chronological sequence. Many of the discourses of the Buddha contain accounts of various episodes in his life. The *Mahaparinibbana Sutta* in particular is a major source for his last year while the *Buddhavamsa* (which is also part of the *Suttapitaka*) gives a very brief account of Gotama's life and the distribution of his relics, together with details of previous Buddhas. Later Buddhist sources attempted to construct a fuller record or 'biography' of the Buddha. Details and a narrative of part of the Buddha's life are contained in the Pali commentaries, especially the *Nidanakatha* compiled by Buddhaghosa in the early 5th century AD. This forms the introduction to the *Jatakatthakatha*, or commentary on the stories of the Buddha's previous lives, and gives an account of the Buddha from his previous life as Sumedha to his Enlightenment and the first two years of his ministry. There are also Sanskrit narratives of his life which are sometimes, as in the case of the 2nd century AD poem by Asvaghosa called *Buddhacarita*, preserved in a fuller form in later Chinese and Tibetan translations. Sir Edwin Arnold's blank-verse epic on the life and teachings of the Buddha, *The Light of Asia* (1884), was based on Sanskrit texts (above all, the *Lalitavistara*) and enjoyed great popularity among English readers in the late 19th century. Many legendary and miraculous features became incorporated into the story of the Buddha's life and local variations developed. The Pali canonical texts and commentaries form the basis of later traditions in Sri Lanka and Southeast Asia where continuous narrative accounts of the Buddha's life were composed, both in Pali and in indigenous languages. Among these were, in Sri Lanka the Pali poem *Jinacarita* and the Sinhalese prose works *Amavatura* and *Pujavaliya* (composed in the 13th century), in Burma the 18th-century *Malalankara vatthu* (*Mala lingara wuthtu*) and the 19th-century *Jinattha-pakasani*, and in Thailand, Laos and Cambodia the *Pathama-sambodhi* (a text of indeterminate age which is known in Thailand as *Pathom Somphot* and exists in its fullest form in a revised edition of 1845). Shining consistently through all the historical accretions and popular imagery of these accounts is the figure of a great religious and moral teacher who inspired a tolerant and lasting system of religious belief and way of life.

Much of the teaching of the Buddha comes from the spiritual ideas, philosophy and social system of the India of his time, but there was much that was new and original. The Buddha taught a way to salvation or deliverance that is open to all to attain and which depends on an individual's own understanding and actions, and not on faith, caste, ritual or divine grace. Salvation is a goal for all Buddhists to strive towards and means attaining in life the state of Nibbana and, when this

Prince Siddhattha sees the four omens.
Or. 14297, f. 10-11, detail.

life ends, achieving Parinibbana or final, complete Nibbana. Some western accounts make no distinction between these terms and Nibbana – which literally means 'blowing out' or 'extinction' but really defies definition – is often rendered as Buddhist heaven, presumably to convey the idea of eternal bliss or salvation. Buddhism, although challenging and reacting to the Brahmanic ideology of ancient India, accepted from the start the concept of rebirth which sees an individual life as one in a successive round of existences (*samsara*) in which each life is conditioned by one's actions (*kamma*; in Sanskrit, *karma*; Burmese, *kan*), that is, the moral value of deeds performed in a previous existence. The Buddha laid emphasis on the intention which lay behind deeds, thoughts and words, and taught that there is every possibility to mould one's *kamma*. It can take countless rebirths for an individual to become what is known as an *arahat* (in Sanskrit, *arhat*), a perfected being who has 'completed the journey' and achieved Nibbana and who will not be reborn. The most feasible path to this otherworldly goal is through the seclusion and discipline of monastic life and the practice of intense spiritual meditation. There are many subjects and levels of meditation, but basically the Buddhist through meditation comes to understand that everything in the world is in a constant state of creation and dissolution, that the self is an illusion and that all sentient existence involves suffering. These concepts of impermanence (*anicca*), of non-self or non-soul (*anatta*) and of the inevitability of suffering (*dukkha*) are central to the Buddha's teaching which offers a path to salvation. The Buddha's Noble Eightfold Path has three components or stages - morality (*sila*), concentration (*samadhi*) and wisdom (*panna*) - which are essential to achieve Nibbana. The Buddha emphasized the importance of self-reliance and it is left to each individual to strive to achieve full intuitive knowledge.

Buddhists in their daily life observe five basic precepts (*panca-sila*): to abstain from killing, from stealing, from engaging in sexual misconduct, from lying, and from taking intoxicants. Additional precepts are observed by monks, nuns and strongly committed laity. Lay people, by providing food and clothing to the monks, by making endowments to the Sangha and by seeking instruction in the Dhamma, can acquire merit and better rebirths. Above all, the Buddha gave to his followers a threefold heritage: first, his own experience and example of perfecting himself; secondly, a new teaching (the Dhamma) about the purpose and meaning of life and the way to salvation; and thirdly, a monastic order (the Sangha) that preserved and spread his teaching and whose way of life exemplifies great merit and virtue. These 'Three Jewels' of Buddhism are relied on as a means to salvation and revered in the thrice repeated Buddhist formula or daily prayer:

> I go to the Buddha for refuge
> I go to the Dhamma for refuge
> I go to the Sangha for refuge.

## *Buddhist art*

Buddhism has over the centuries inspired many artistic masterpieces. The figure of the Buddha did not appear in very early Buddhist art (prior to the 1st century AD) and symbols were used to indicate his presence and key events in his life. Thus, his Enlightenment was represented by a Bodhi tree (the sacred fig tree under which he meditated), his first sermon by a wheel (the 'wheel of the law' - his doctrines), his years of wandering and ministry by a footprint, and his death (Parinibbana) by a stupa. These symbols can be found in reliefs from Bharhut, Sanchi and Amaravati in India. When images of the Buddha in human form did appear - first in the art of Gandhara and Mathura - the iconography and the hand gestures (in Sankrit, *mudra*) of the Buddha were of great significance. Tradition states that the Buddha was born with 32 major auspicious signs or marks on his body, as well as many minor ones, and artists, in seeking to represent these, imparted certain characteristics common to most Buddha images, although regional variations in style and preferred models and gestures naturally developed. Among the most noteworthy iconographic features of Buddha images are the cranial bump (*usnisa*) indicating wisdom, the long earlobes and signs on the hands and the feet, while a large repertoire of gestures serves to symbolize and communicate particular incidents in his life and messages. Thus, images of the Buddha seated cross-legged with his hands in his lap indicate meditation, while those with the right hand touching the ground near his right knee refer to the Buddha's calling the earth to witness when challenged by evil forces; the hands held in front of the chest, the right palm outward with the thumb and forefinger forming a circle which is touched by the outstretched middle finger of the left hand represents the preaching of the first sermon; images of the reclining or sleeping Buddha represent the Parinibbana. In time a form of narrative sculpture developed of which the most famous examples are the Gandhara reliefs of Pakistan and Afghanistan which date from the 1st to 4th centuries AD, and those of the 8th-9th century AD temple of Borobudur in central Java. Some ancient temples were also decorated with wall paintings depicting events in the life of the Buddha, although many have not survived the passage of time or have been repeatedly painted over. Modern Buddhist temples still continue this practice, while some now also feature life-size tableaux and even moving mechanical figures. The spiritual inspiration that so infused early Buddhist art seems by the 19th and 20th century to have become less sublime and styles more secular, but the motivating force of acquiring merit remains unchanged and ensures continued patronage and production of Buddhist art.

## Burmese manuscript art

Burma, one of the most strongly Buddhist countries in the world today, has a long tradition of narrative representations of the Buddha's life. Many of the Buddhist temples in Burma's ancient capital, Pagan, which flourished from the 11th to the 13th century AD contain sculptured friezes and plaques as well as wall paintings of episodes from the Buddha's life. These, apart from their aesthetic qualities, were supremely religious in purpose and primarily concerned with communicating the message of the Buddha at a time when the Theravada form of Buddhism was gaining ascendancy in Burma under King Anawrahta (1044-77) and his successors. As in Indian Buddhist art, in some Burmese temple decorations certain principal events of the Buddha's life (and also of his previous lives) were compressed with great skill and sophistication into a single scene, with associated figures and symbols grouped around. This format also featured on the small Indian-style terracotta votive tablets or plaques that were particularly popular at Pagan. It is not known when the first Burmese manuscripts illustrating the Buddha's life appeared as few pre-18th century manuscripts have survived, but certainly by the 19th century series of manuscripts illustrating both the life of the Buddha and the *Jataka* stories of the Buddha's previous lives were being produced in some abundance. Moreover, as a subject for manuscript illustration, the life of the Buddha was especially popular in Burma, apparently far more so than in such other Theravada Buddhist countries as Sri Lanka and Thailand which have produced relatively few examples of this genre. It is possible that the production and popularity of illustrated life of the Buddha manu-

Prince Siddhattha cutting off his hair.
Or. 14297, f. 12, detail.

Concertina format and front cover of the Burney MS.
Or. 14297

scripts in Burma is linked to the compilation in Burmese of the first full prose account of the Buddha's life. This work, *Mala lingara wutbtu*, was completed at Amarapura in 1798 by the monk, Dutiya Medi Hsayadaw (1747-1834) who also bore several titles, of which the best known is Kawiwunthabidaza. Once the story of the Buddha's life was rendered into Burmese, it became more accessible than in its Pali version – knowledge of Pali being largely confined to monks and scholars – and challenged artists' imagination with more details and events to depict. Some manuscripts bear on their covers the title of this work, although the text running beneath the pictures inside is not the full text, but an abbreviated form narrating the essence of the story of the Buddha's life and elucidating the episodes depicted. Other manuscripts which form part of a series on the life of the Buddha simply state on the cover the part number and an indication of the first and last events depicted in the manuscript. There is no rigid, set pattern of scenes in Burmese life of the Buddha manuscripts. Obviously, certain key events are included, while the choice and depiction of other episodes in the Buddha's long life can vary greatly from one manuscript to another in accordance, presumably, with the textual sources followed and the individual predilections of the commissioner of the manuscript and the talents of the artists.

Before turning to a more detailed description of the two manuscripts featured in this book, some introduction to Burmese manuscripts in general is needed. There are two main types of manuscripts: those written on oblong strips of palm leaves (called *pe-za* in Burmese), and those on long sheets of paper, folded concertina fashion, to make a folding book (called *parabaik* in Burmese). Palm leaf manuscripts of the Pali canonical texts and Buddhist commentaries predominate, while legal, historical and literary texts were also recorded on palm leaf. Paper *parabaik*s can be either black or natural creamy-white colour. The black-paper *parabaik*s were less long lasting than the white *parabaik*s and were mostly used as notebooks and for draft administrative records, the text being written on them in white soapstone or steatite. Sometimes they were used to record astrological and tattooing designs, and for sketch maps. White-paper *parabaik*s were written on in ink and used for a variety of purposes, above all for painted illustrations, in which case the paper was usually first given a chalky white or pale-coloured background wash. Common subjects for illustration were the life of the Buddha, the *Jataka* stories of the Buddha's previous lives, court scenes and entertainments, cosmology, and classificatory works depicting types of elephants, royal barges, military manoeuvres, objects in use at the royal court, and such like. Covers of the folding books were often stiffened and some decorated with gilding and raised patterns or inlaid coloured glass, or tooled leather, or painted geometric designs. Occasionally, the title or subject of the work and, more rarely, details of the commissioner or donor of the manuscript would be inscribed on the covers. If opened out fully, a *parabaik* can extend to several metres, but they were not really designed to be viewed all at once, but opening by opening, and were kept folded up and stored in manuscript chests.

Painted *parabaik*s have great visual impact, with brilliantly coloured and richly gilded scenes flowing across each opening and onto the next. Their composition bears some relationship to that of wall paintings and indeed scenes in Burmese *parabaik*s look as if they have been transferred from a temple wall onto, and overspilling, the folds of the manuscript. Manuscript painters had, however, access to a brighter palette than is found in wall paintings, and embellished their work with gilding. Rough practice sketches sometimes found on the reverse sides of illustrated folding books give a clue to the artists' working methods. Outlines are first drawn in red or brown, and the colour then filled in, the whole having a flat, linear appearance. Scenes generally flow from left to right, although events are not necessarily painted in order of occurrence since scenes separated in time can be grouped together if they share the same location. Sometimes the division of scenes is made naturalistically by lines of trees or buildings, or by rows of figures who play some part in the narrative. The curlicued double borders which surround and divide scenes in some 18th-century wall paintings are not found in manuscript paintings. Gilding is used to decorate the tiered spires of palace buildings (which are further highlighted by being placed against plain dark blocks of colour), and also to embellish the robes of royalty and courtiers, and, above all, for the figure of the Buddha. This convention is extended in illustrations of the *Jataka* stories to gilding whatever creature (an elephant, a bird, a deer, etc.) or personage the Buddha had been in a former reincarnation. There is in early painted *parabaik*s no central or coordinated perspective, but rather multiple perspectives, so that events inside and outside buildings can be viewed simultaneously. The device of a horizon is not much used in earlier paintings, but occasionally appears near the top of the composition. Some depth is provided by the practice of painting key figures and buildings against a solid dark background, often of piled-up swirling rocks. A lower horizon and receding, diminishing perspectives became increasingly common in later 19th- century paintings, when also a more centred composition began to appear. Such features presumably reflect the influence of western techniques and the trained 'company school' style of Indian painters working for the East India Company. All British diplomatic missions to Burma employed artists to record scenes and events. Michael Symes, in his account of his 1795 embassy to Burma, specifically mentions the interest shown by the Burmese king in the accurate and realistic representations produced by Symes' Indian painter, Singey Bey, who was asked to produce for the king a painting of the Buddha and to copy another of elephants. Burmese court artists may also have seen illustrations in western books, while later in the 19th century King Thibaw actually employed some Italian artists. Nor can the influence of Thai artists, brought back to Burma after the conquest of the Thai capital of Ayutthaya in 1767, be discounted. As the 19th century progressed, however, much of the individuality and verve that characterizes earlier Burmese manuscript paintings was lost and scenes became more static and rigid with rows of bland-faced and repetitive figures, set in simple landscapes or in proportioned interiors. It is a feature of all Burmese life of the Buddha and *Jataka* paintings that the artist drew freely on his contemporary surroundings, and made no attempt to portray the Buddha in an historical Indian setting. This can result in such charming incongruities as the Bodhisatta travelling in a paddle steamer. It also, of course, provides valuable clues for dating the paintings by such details as hairstyles, costumes and architecture and, above all, a wonderful evocation of life in Burma before the British annexation of Upper Burma put an end to a proudly independent Buddhist kingdom in 1885-86.

## *The Burney* parabaiks

The two Burmese manuscripts on which this book is based were selected for three reasons: their interesting provenance, artistic merit and their compact presentation of the story of the Buddha. Many other illustrated life of the Buddha manuscripts run into several volumes which have, in the course of time, become dispersed so that a complete sequence cannot be assembled from the collection of a single institution or library. The manuscripts (Or. 14297 and Or. 14298 in the Oriental and India Office Collections of the British Library) were once owned by the British diplomat and orientalist Henry Burney (1792-1845), who was British Resident at the Burmese Court of Ava from 1830 to 1837. They were acquired by the British Library in 1985 from a descendant of Henry Burney, but the family had no record or memory of the circumstances in which the manuscripts came into their possession. Over and above the family link, Henry Burney's ownership of these manuscripts is, however, independently confirmed by documents in the Library of the Royal Commonwealth Society, London. Among the Royal Commonwealth Society's collection of Burney Papers is a 26-page document in Burney's hand, entitled 'Description of Pictures of Boodh'. This document (listed B IX in the MS catalogue of the RCS Burney Papers, and written on East India Company paper watermarked E Wise, 1829) describes the first 24 openings of Or. 14297, each of which is identified in the notes by numbers and letters ('a', 'b' 'c', etc.) which correspond to those marked in ink by Burney on the actual manuscripts, and contains a translation and commentary upon the Burmese text. Burney does not appear to have completed his description and study of the manuscripts or, if he did, the rest of his notes describing the remainder of Or. 14297 and its sequel (Or.14298) have not survived. Unlike several other of Burney's documents in the Royal Commonwealth Society, his draft notes were certainly not subsequently published as an article in any learned journal of the time. His notes reveal that his primary interest was in understanding in some depth Buddhist teachings and in identifying each scene in the Buddha's life. His willingness to write in ink on the pages of the manuscripts would also seem to indicate that their art was only of secondary interest to him. Another document (listed as H XI in the MS catalogue of the RCS Burney Papers) and entitled 'List of Burmese Books collected at Ava' includes the entry 'Malalengara, Good Works or Life of Gaudama' and this could well refer to the two illustrated manuscripts of the life of the Buddha. It is disappointing, however, that Burney's papers throw no light on the manuscripts' creation nor on the circumstances in which he acquired them. His journal, which unfortunately only covers his first two years in Burma (1830-32), provides no clue. Burney was exceptionally adept at learning oriental languages and within two years of his arrival at the Burmese capital he was able to do without official interpreters in his dealings with the Burmese court and had read the voluminous Burmese chronicles and many other Burmese texts. His fluency in

Queen Mahamaya's procession.
Or. 14297, f. 6, detail.

Burmese and his understanding of Burmese history, religion and culture enabled him to establish unusually good relations with King Bagyidaw (1819-37) and his ministers. Burney made a collection of Burmese black *parabaik*s, many of which were copies of Burmese official documents recording discussions held between Burney and high Burmese officials, and which were supplied by them to him as a mark of goodwill. Burney's collection of black *parabaik*s is also in the British Library, having been deposited in the old India Office Library some 150 years ago together with the official proceedings of Burney's mission. Burney had an especially high regard for the minister called Myawaddy Min Gyi U Sa (1766-1853?) who was an important figure at the court of King Bagyidaw. U Sa was a cultivated man of letters and it is tempting to speculate that his conversations with Burney could have turned to Buddhism and art, and that the illustrated manuscripts of the life of the Buddha may have been presented to him by some such influential person at the royal court. Furthermore, it is known that U Sa was a patron and supporter of the Dutiya Medi Hsayadaw – the author of the Burmese prose version of the life of the Buddha (*Mala lingara wuthtu*) – and indeed built and endowed a monastery for him at Ava. It is possible that U Sa, inspired by the learned monk's great work, may himself have commissioned the manuscript paintings based on it. To take speculation even further, U Sa may even have subsequently presented these precious *parabaik*s to Burney, perhaps for safekeeping during the turmoil accompanying King Bagyidaw's overthrow, a period when U Sa himself was for a short time imprisoned. Burney assessed U Sa as 'by far the most intelligent and best informed minister' and noted that he was 'fond of kulas' (– *kala* being a Burmese term for foreigners). Another, but even less likely, candidate might be the Mekkhara Prince, an uncle of King Bagyidaw, who had learnt English and translated into Burmese articles from Rees' Cyclopaedia. The Prince was described by Burney as 'an extraordinary character' and as 'very curious on subjects of science and philosophy' and he enjoyed conversations with Burney and other foreigners on scientific matters, but remained, in Burney's words, 'very timid and afraid of becoming too intimate with the Residency'. An even more intriguing, but very remote, possibility is that Burney himself might have commissioned the manuscripts.

Burney's possession of the manuscripts does at least provide a definite cut-off date for their production, that is, pre-1837 (the date when Burney withdrew the British Residency from Ava to Rangoon in the aftermath of a royal coup d'état which brought King Tharrawaddy to the throne). This is obviously helpful in terms of dating Burmese painted manuscripts and artistic styles. Study of the style and details of the Burney life of the Buddha manuscripts and comparison with other examples of this genre and with dated wall paintings suggest that the Burney parabaiks can be dated to between the late 1790s and the 1830s, and most probably to the early 1800s. This ranks the Burney manuscripts among the earliest surviving illustrated manuscripts from Burma. The great majority of extant painted *parabaik*s date from the Mandalay period (1857-85). Tantalisingly little is known about the painters who produced so many masterpieces of Burmese manuscript art. The Burmese chronicles name many painters who worked under royal patronage at the Burmese court, but individual manuscripts are very rarely signed or dated and were often worked on by teams of artists, with varying degrees of skill.

Burney's two manuscripts are fine and rare examples of Burmese art. Although differing in page dimensions and extent (Or. 14297 measures 49 x 19 cm, 19.3 x 7.5 inches, and has 104 folds with illustrations on 52 openings; Or. 14298 measures 47.3 x 19 cm, 18.6 x 7.5 inches, and has 49 folds with illustrations on 25 openings), they are painted by the same hand(s) and planned as an entity, the one being a continuation of the other. Sixty of the two manuscripts' total of 77 illustrated openings or folds are reproduced in this book. The Burmese text is written in ink in a yellow border running across the bottom of the pages - (the English text that replaces it of necessity occupies a wider border than in the original manuscripts) - and, compared with other manuscripts, is written in a surprisingly poor hand. The Burney *parabaik*s are remarkable not only for their skilled and compact rendition of the long life of the Buddha, but for their unusual and beautifully painted covers. Each cover bears a different figure, now - as might be expected - somewhat worn and rubbed, whose identity may also hold a clue to the commissioner or donor of the manuscripts. The top and bottom covers of Or.14297 are each decorated with a painting of a white robed deity who probably represent the gods Sakka and Brahma while the covers of Or. 14298 - illustrated in this book on pages 19 and 80 - each has a figure in coloured robes, possibly representing two of the four guardian gods of the world (*lokapala*). The figures are depicted with hands joined in reverence and the whole can be taken to represent the homage and submission of the gods to the Buddha. Another possible interpretation is that the white-robed figure (who can be seen in the illustration of Or. 14297 on page 10) represents the Burmese monarch who traditionally donned the royal Sakka robes for the propitiation ceremony of Sakka and Brahma and on other religious and ceremonial occasions. The association of the Burmese monarch with Sakka, king of the gods, and with the Buddha is longstanding - some kings claimed they were themselves future Buddhas - and the king's throne within the great audience hall of the royal palace echoed the gods' heavenly splendours. The palace architecture and the symbolism employed in its decoration proclaim and emphasize this, as did all royal ceremony and the whole annual cycle of religious festivals and ceremonies observed at the Burmese court. Throughout the manuscripts, the kings and the great gods are depicted in identical three-tiered costumes and it is easy to see that the Burmese king or high royal official under whose patronage the manuscripts were painted was associating himself with the merit of the kings and gods who ministered to and revered the great lord Buddha.

## Artistic style

Detailed notes on the Buddhist context and art of each opening of the Burney manuscripts illustrated on the following pages are given in the Appendix, but some general stylistic points concerning the depiction of figures throughout the manuscripts are worth making here. Faces are outlined in reddish-brown, nearly always in three-quarters profile, with the pupils in the corners of the lidded eyes; eyebrows are drawn in black and either short and round or arched; noses are straight and the single line of the nose drawn in an unbroken line from the eyebrow; mouths have a curved upper lip and, not joined, a straight lower lip, with a third shorter stroke between the lip and the chinline; there are usually two lines at the neck. Palace ladies wear tight short bodice wrappers (Burmese, *yin-zi*), long skirts (Burmese, *htamein*) which trail on the ground, patterned from the hips down with horizontal undulating zig-zag patterns (Burmese, *acheik*) in yellow, green, red and white; over this they wear a diaphanous long sleeved top reaching to the hips, and a long coloured flowered or spangled shawl (*pawa*) draped across the level of the bosom, with ends trailing behind, or sometimes knotted to one side. The women's long hair is worn in a low knotted bun at the nape of the neck, with two (sometimes three) strands of hair coming forward above the ear and across the cheek. Men wear their long topknots of hair protruding forwards and tied round several times in various styles with a circlet of cloth. Their long lower garments (Burmese, *pahso*) are striped or chequered in pattern and they sometimes wear a white diaphanous overshirt which falls at the sides to their hips. The court and royal costumes as well as those of the deities are much more elaborate and painted with careful attention to detail – items of dress, ornaments and insignia all being prescribed according to detailed sumptuary regulations. Burmese artists have always excelled in the depiction of elephants, but the Burney manuscripts also have accomplished portrayals of horses and other animals, often with expressive faces. Another feature is the decorative insertion of various small birds who perch in carefully painted trees or swoop through the skies.

## The life of the Buddha in other manuscripts

Not all episodes of the Buddha's life are represented in the Burney manuscripts, while some episodes are given fuller, and some shorter, treatment than in other life of the Buddha manuscripts. Of necessity too, in selecting 60 openings for reproduction in this book in 30 double page spreads, some scenes from the Burney manuscripts have had to be omitted. By reproducing below (see pages 16-17) scenes from other life of the Buddha manuscripts in the British Library, some of the gaps can be filled and at the same time comparisons made between Burmese styles. Four principal events in the life of the Buddha – his birth, enlightenment, the first sermon and his death (entry into Parinibbana) – are always represented, and indeed these are of primary importance in Buddhist art worldwide, while the sites of these occurrences are major places of Buddhist pilgrimage. Burmese artists are particularly fond of depicting the 'Great Renunciation' or departure scene when the Buddha-to-be takes a last look at his sleeping wife and child and rides out of the palace to begin his quest for Supreme Enlightenment. This scene is magnificently depicted in another British Library manuscript, Or. 4762, which is the third in a series illustrating the Buddha's life.

The great renunciation. Or.4762, f. 3-4.

The encounter with Mara. Or.4762, f. 5-6.

The defeat of the heretics. Or. 5757, f. 11-12.

Prince Siddhattha's departure.   Or. 14197, f. 12b-13.

Jivaka the physician is called to treat the Buddha.
Or. 14405, f. 22b-23.

 မြတ်ဘုရားသခင်ကိုဒွေမ္မားပင့်ပူဇော်ပုံ။    အာပွါလိက္ကာမာသဂုဏ်တော်ဘုရည်းကိုလ္လူဟဲ့။    ဘုရးသခင်သဿသဂုဏ်တော်ဉ်ရည်း

Ambapali's donation. Or. 13534, f. 18-19.

Compared with the Burney *parabaik*'s rather crowded version of this scene (see pages 28-29), the painter has produced a rich and flowing composition of this key scene and, unlike the Burney manuscript, has shown the gods muffling with their hands the sound of the horse's hooves and, on another opening (illustrated on page 16), his encounter with Mara, Spirit of Evil. A similar, but less accomplished treatment is found in another manuscript, Or. 14197, which throughout is painted with meticulous attention to detail (– note the post-1857 Mandalay city multi-tiered gateway –) but lacks the vitality of the Burney and other early 19th century life of the Buddha manuscripts. Certain miraculous events in the Buddha's life are associated with the city of Savatthi and include the Buddha's confounding of the 'wrong believers' or heretics where the Buddha caused a mango tree in flower and fruit to appear instantly (although the heretics had cut down all trees because the Buddha had announced that he would display his powers at the foot of a mango tree), and his performance of the twin miracle (or miracle of the pairs – of fire and water) where he walked in the air while emitting flames and waves. Soon after, the Buddha ascended to Tavatimsa heaven to preach to his mother and to the gods, and then returned to earth by a triple stairway. The twin miracle is represented in the Burney *parabaik* on just one side of a fold (Or. 14297, f.42b), but is not reproduced in this book, while the mango tree incident does not appear in the Burney manuscripts at all. It is, however, depicted fully in another British Library manuscript, Or. 5757, the eleventh in the same series as Or. 4762. In this, dark-skinned heretics are shown chopping down trees, but the Buddha is offered a ripe mango by Ganda, the gardener of the king of Savatthi. The Buddha eats the mango and tells Ganda to plant the stone and water it, whereupon a huge mango tree springs up covered in flowers and fruit. The confusion of the heretics who are scattered by a great whirlwind and flee in every direction, while one casts himself into the water and drowns, is depicted with great vigour in Or. 5757. Also omitted from the Burney *parabaik*s is the story of Jivaka who at a very early age showed great skill in medicine and effected many cures and became a royal physician and attended the Buddha. Or. 14405 in the British Library contains extensive sequences depicting Jivaka and the cases he treated. The manuscript throughout is brightly gilded and finely painted in the Mandalay period (1857-85) style. As in most mid and late 19th-century manuscripts, scenes are separated by vertical yellow borders, with an altogether more spacious, less crowded composition than in earlier manuscripts. In the last year of his life, the Buddha was at Vesali where he accepted the invitation of a celebrated courtesan, Ambapali, to feed him and his monks, in preference to the invitation of more noble personages. Afterwards, Ambapali presented her mango grove to the Buddha for his use. This scene is depicted in a late 19th-century manuscript, Or. 13534. In this, the folds of the Buddha's red robe are picked out in gold, his feet rest upon an elaborate lotus base and each scene is presented from a more central viewpoint. Although the interiors of the buildings are carefully observed and painted, the figures are lifeless and, when kneeling in reverence, appear on the verge of overbalancing. The white borders and reduction of the text to a brief caption is typical of later manuscripts. From these other manuscript scenes, shown here in chronological order of composition (and all later than the Burney manuscripts), something can be glimpsed of the considerable variation in styles of Burmese life of the Buddha manuscripts over a period of less than a century and of the richness of Burma's manuscript traditions.

*Right* Painted front cover of Or. 14298

The most excellent Bodhisatta, the Buddha-to-be, who surpasses the humans, gods and Brahmas of the three worlds was, an innumerable number of existences past, an ascetic named Sumedha. At that time, Dipankara Buddha had been invited by the king to a feast and Sumedha lay across a muddy patch of unfinished road on the way to the palace so that the Buddha might tread over his body with-

out soiling his feet. Marvelling at Sumedha's great determination, Dipankara Buddha proclaimed that Sumedha too would become a Buddha after acquiring and practising the Ten Perfections and their associated Thirty Virtues, together with the Five Great Charities and the Three Good Works throughout an immeasurable period of world cycles.

In his last human existence before that in which he became the Buddha, the Bodhisatta was born as Prince Vessantara, son of King Sanjaya in the city of Jetuttara of the kingdom of Sivirattha. Now Prince Vessantara gave away in charity the kingdom's white elephant and became a hermit on Van-kagiri mountain. Furthermore, while there he did not shrink from giving away his children to the brahmin Jujaka. After this life of perfect generosity as Prince Vessantara, he was reborn as Setaketu in Tusita heaven. There, all the gods of the ten thousand universes came to petition him to become a

Buddha in the human world and he therefore considered and chose the five points or circumstances of a Buddha appearing: in what epoch, in which continent, at what place, and of what race and to which mother should he be born? And so Queen Mahamaya of the Sakyan city of Kapilavatthu conceived the future Buddha and was protected in her chamber by the four great kings, guardian gods of the four quarters of the world.

Queen Mahamaya, having carried the future Buddha in her womb for ten months as smoothly as oil in a monk's bowl, submitted her desire to visit relatives in the country of Devadaha to King Suddhodana who granted her permission to proceed on her way, borne in a golden palanquin and surrounded by attendants. Between the countries of Kapilavatthu and Devadaha in a beautiful grove of flowering sala trees called Lumbini, the Queen was delivered, stretching out her hand and holding the branch of a sala tree which was bending towards her. At that moment, the great Brahmas received the infant in a golden net, the four guardian gods on a black antelope skin and the royal ministers on a fine white royal cloth. The infant then stood on the ground and, taking seven paces to the north, spoke the words: 'I am the most exalted and excellent'. That same day the holy man Kalade-

vala, who could see whatever had happened in forty previous worlds and whatever would happen in forty future worlds, came to the palace to behold the Buddha-to-be. The child, on being carried near to pay reverence, raised both feet and placed them on the braided hair of the holy man, who smiled because he saw the Prince would become a Buddha and wept because he himself would not live to see that event. On the fifth day after the birth, Kondanna, who was the youngest of eight brahmins versed in the interpretation of signs, held up one finger – meaning that the child would surely become a Buddha – while the other brahmins each held up two fingers, meaning that the child would either become a Buddha or a world emperor.

A month after the birth of the Buddha-to-be, his father the King went out to perform the royal ploughing ceremony. The child was placed in the shade of a rose-apple tree and entered into the first state of meditation, during which time the shadow of the tree did not change or move. On hearing of this wonder, King Suddhodana came and paid homage to his son. As the young Prince grew, the royal tutor soon found that his pupil was beyond his instruction. His father built him three palaces, one for each season, and the Prince was entertained royally and passed his days in luxury and com-

fort, shielded from the harsh realities of life, for his father wished only that his son should become a great ruler of this world. When he was sixteen years old, Prince Siddhattha Gotama displayed his skills in archery to an assembly of his kinsmen so that none could question his mastery of the traditional arts. At the same age he married Princess Yasodhara who was the daughter of King Suddhodana's brother-in-law, King Suppabuddha, and who had been born on the same day as the Prince. And the marriage was celebrated with great feasting, entertainments and rejoicing.

One day, when Prince Siddhattha set out for the royal gardens, he encountered the Four Great Signs: an old man, a sick man, a corpse, and a monk. And, when he thus learnt of old age, disease, and death, his mind became agitated by the miseries of this world. On arriving at the gardens, he seated himself upon a large smooth stone and felt a desire to put on his royal ornaments, whereupon a god, assuming the appearance of a royal valet, came down from the upper world to adorn him. At that moment, the Prince's courtiers came and reported to him the birth of a son. Returning to the city in the cool of the evening, the Prince in all his splendour was greeted by the Princess Kisagotami with the joyful words: 'Happy and calm today is the mind of the mother, the father and the wife who has such a lord'. Her words brought to the prince's mind the thought that only when the fires of

attachment, hatred and delusion are extinguished can one be truly happy. He resolved henceforth to seek the calm of Nibbana, and taking off his pearl necklace, he presented it to the Princess. On his return to the palace, all the dancers, musicians and singers came immediately to entertain the Prince, but his mind was free of worldly passion and he fell asleep. When he awoke, he saw the palace ladies asleep with their hair and dress dishevelled, some dribbling, some grinding their teeth, some talking in their sleep and some snoring, and his palace seemed to him like a charnel-house of loathsome dead bodies. So taking one last look at his sleeping wife and child, he summoned the nobleman Channa, mounted his white horse Kanthaka and, with Channa holding onto its tail, rode out of the palace, with the gods muffling the sound of the horse's hooves.

Outside the gates, Mara, the Spirit of Evil, barred his way and tried to deter Prince Siddhattha from leaving to seek Enlightenment in the solitude of the wilderness. The Prince wanted to take one last look at the city of Kapilavatthu, but thought he should resist such a desire whereupon the whole earth turned, like a potter's wheel, before his eyes. In a single day the Prince passed through three kingdoms and came to the great river Anoma some thirty yojana, or leagues, distant from his father's palace. The Prince crossed the river with one leap of his horse and dismounted on its bank of silvery sand. Then, taking his long topknot of hair in his left hand and his sword in his right, the Bodhisatta cut off his hair with one stroke. Casting it upwards, he said, 'If I am truly to become a Buddha, let this

hair ascend into the sky, and, if not, let it fall to the ground', and the hair was caught by the god Sakka in a gold flowered casket and enshrined in Tavatimsa heaven. At that time, the Brahma named Ghatikara appeared and offered to the Bodhisatta the eight things necessary for a monk (which are the three robes, an alms bowl, a razor, a needle, a water strainer and a girdle). The Bodhisatta put on the robes of a monk and ordered Channa and the horse to return to the palace. Kanthaka the horse was so distressed to be sent back that he died of grief on the spot, and Channa, sobbing, set out alone to give news of the Prince to his family.

After spending seven days in the grove of mango trees called Anupiya, the Bodhisatta proceeded in one day to the city of Rajagaha in the kingdom of Magadha some thirty leagues distant and decided to enter the city in the manner of former Buddhas – that is, with his alms bowl to receive offerings of food. His appearance caused such excitement and commotion in the city that King Bimbisara was informed of it and decided to have the stranger followed to see who he was and if he ate all the mix-

ture of food put in his alms bowl. The Bodhisatta went to the foot of Pandava hill and, overcoming his repugnance at the contents of the bowl, was able to eat. When this was reported to him, King Bimbisara made haste to visit and talk to the Bodhisatta and, discerning that he would assuredly become a Buddha, Bimbisara requested that his kingdom should be the first to be visited by the Bodhisatta once he had attained Enlightenment. This the Bodhisatta agreed to do.

Continuing on his travels, the Bodhisatta learnt in the forest of Uruvela all that the hermits Alara and Uddaka could teach him. Then for six years in the jungle he practised many religious austerities, including extreme fasting, with five wandering ascetics as his attendants. But such practices, he concluded, were not the path to Enlightenment. In those days in a village called Senani there lived Sujata, the daughter of a rich man. Sujata's request (to have a son) which she had made at the foot of

a banyan tree had been fulfilled and so she prepared as a special thank-offering to the tree's guardian spirit some rice boiled in concentrated milk whilst Sakka, Brahma and other gods kept watch and infused the milk with heavenly flavours. She then carried  some of the milk-rice in a precious golden bowl to the tree under which the Bodhisatta was seated in meditation and the Bodhisatta, stretching out his hand, received Sujata's offering.

The Bodhisatta divided Sujata's offering of milk-rice into forty-nine mouthfuls which thereupon he ate on the banks of the river Neranjara, and then set the golden bowl afloat, saying 'If I am truly to become a Buddha today, may this bowl float upstream'. This it did and then sank to the abode of the serpent king, Mahakala, where it knocked against the bowls of three previous Buddhas and roused the serpent king who bestowed praises upon the Bodhisatta. After setting the golden bowl afloat, the Bodhisatta remained in the forest of sala trees near the Neranjara river until the cool of the evening

when he went down to the Bodhi tree along a road prepared and adorned by the gods. On the way he met a grass cutter named Sotthiya who offered him eight handfuls of grass. These he scattered on the ground by the east side of the tree whereupon a throne fourteen cubits high appeared. Sakka, Brahma, and all the greater and lesser gods offered homage and worship with conch shell, white umbrella, yak's tail and circular fans, and harp music.

Whilst the Bodhisatta was seated cross-legged on the Aparajita ('unconquered') throne from which he had resolved not to arise until he attained Enlightenment, Mara, the Spirit of Evil, mounted on the mighty elephant Girimekhala came to make war upon him using nine different kinds of weapons. But the Bodhisatta's accumulated perfections, culminating in the virtue of generosity which he had practised in his existence as Prince Vessantara caused the defeat of Mara and his army, while the earth itself trembled and testified to the Bodhisatta's fitness to be the Fully Enlightened One. During the first watch of the night the Bodhisatta meditated and obtained the power of seeing all former states of existence; at midnight he obtained the divine vision possessed by perfect ones; during the

third watch of the night he realised the Four Truths. And so, being endowed with the Ten Strengths and the Four Points of Confidence and with every other quality necessary to become a Buddha, and having attained the highest stage on the path of perfection and perfect omniscience, at dawn he attained Enlightenment, becoming a Buddha of whom there is no equal in the three worlds of men, gods and Brahmas. When this great wonder took place, ten thousand worlds were shaken twelve times and echoed with the words 'Most Excellent Being', and Sakka, Brahmas and gods, garudas and nagas appeared to pay reverence to the perfect Buddha, from whom light radiated in multi-colour streams.

The whole universe was as if covered with beautiful flowers and for forty-nine days the Buddha's mind remained deeply engaged in sublime contemplation as he meditated in seven different places. Throughout this time he took no food, nor experienced the least want, and his appearance and countenance stayed unchanged. For seven successive days he remained seated in meditation on the Aparajita throne. He then came down from the throne and, going a certain distance, stood looking at

the Bodhi tree for a further seven days with a steadfast, unblinking gaze. For the next seven days, the Buddha walked to and fro along a golden walkway built by the gods between the throne and the spot called Animisa ('unblinking') where he had before stood looking at the seat of Enlightenment. For the following seven days he contemplated the seven books of the Abhidhamma in Ratanaghara, a beautiful jewelled house which shone like gold.

Next he went to the Ajapala ('goatherds') banyan tree. Whilst seated in meditation under it, the Buddha was first visited by the three daughters of Mara who endeavoured in vain to seduce him by assuming various guises, and then by a haughty brahmin named Huhunka who questioned him on the nature of true brahmins. For the next period of seven days the Buddha went to a tree near the lake of Mucalinda. During these seven days there was violent rain and the serpent king Mucalinda sheltered the Buddha by winding his coils seven times round the Buddha and spreading his hood over the Buddha's head. The Buddha next remained seated for seven days under the Rajayatana tree

to the south of the Bodhi tree, experiencing the bliss of emancipation. At the end of this time, Sakka, King of the Gods, presented him with the fruit of the myrobalan tree, a tooth-stick from the stem of a betel creeper and water from the lake of Anotatta for his refreshment. Next, the four great guardian gods presented him with four bowls which the Buddha miraculously caused to become one bowl with four rims, and in this bowl the Buddha then received the offerings of rice cakes cooked in honey tendered by the two brothers Tapussa and Bhallika, merchants from the distant city of Ukka-lapa in Ramanna.

Now, returning to the Ajapala tree, the Buddha hesitated as to whether he should preach his teachings (the Dhamma) at all. Then Sahampati, the great Brahma of the Brahma heavens, and many gods, all came to petition the Buddha to preach to mankind. And when the Buddha considered to whom he should first preach, he thought first of Alara and Uddaka, but upon perceiving that they had recently died, he next saw that his former companions, the five wandering ascetics, were in a deer park near Benares and he resolved to preach first to them. On the way there, he encountered the false priest Upaka and announced to him that he had attained Enlightenment. On seeing the Buddha approach them the five ascetics at first were determined to pay him no regard since he had abandoned the practice of austerities, but they were unable to keep their resolve and came to meet him.

And so in the deer park at Isipatana near Benares the Buddha preached his first sermon which is called the Dhammacakkappavattana sutta, or the setting of the wheel of the Dhamma in motion, which contained the fundamental principles of his teaching, expressed as the Four Noble Truths: life is full of suffering; the cause of suffering is desire; cessation of desire ends suffering; and the way to end suffering is to follow the Noble Eightfold Path of right views, right aims, right speech, right action, right livelihood, right effort, right mindfulness, and right concentration. Thus, on the full moon day, all the gods and Brahmas heard the Buddha's message and the five ascetics became his first disciples. And whilst the Buddha was in the deer park the memorable conversion of a young layman took place.

There was in the city of Benares a rich man's son named Yasa who led a life of pleasure surrounded by singers and dancing girls until one day he suddenly resolved to subdue his passions and become a monk. It was then that the father of Yasa invited the Buddha to his house and made him offerings of food, and when Yasa's family heard the Buddha's preaching they all became his lay disciples and supporters. After Yasa became a monk, his example was followed by his four close friends and by other

friends and companions so that the Buddha now had sixty disciples. At first a true follower was accepted by the Buddha with the simple words 'Ehi bhikkhu' ('come, O monk'), but later rules came to be established. The Buddha told his monk-disciples to go forth in different directions to preach his teachings and advised them on the admittance of followers into the Sangha or community of monks that was forming. The Buddha then continued on his way alone.

The Buddha, upon coming to Uruvela grove where lived three hermit brothers and their many followers, requested permission from the elder brother, Uruvela-Kassapa, to spend the night there and
Kassapa replied that he was welcome to stay in his cook-house, but that he should beware the
poisonous Naga (serpent) which guarded it. The Buddha, however, had no fear and when the Naga
in the night threatened him by sending forth smoke and flames, the Buddha displayed his superior

powers. When morning came, the Buddha caught the Naga and put him in his alms bowl and showed him to Kassapa who was impressed and invited the Buddha to stay on in Uruvela grove. While the Buddha stayed at Uruvela grove many miraculous happenings occurred, but for a long time the hermit brother Uruvela-Kassapa persisted in thinking that the Buddha was not even his equal.

On one occasion, Kassapa invited the Buddha to come and partake of his meal and the Buddha agreed, saying that he would come and join him later. The Buddha then went and plucked the golden jambu fruit from the farthest extremity of Jambudipa, the southern continent of man, and yet reached the eating place before Kassapa. When Kassapa arrived, the Buddha offered him the fruit, but Kassapa acknowledged it was not suitable for him to eat it. On another occasion, the Buddha wanted to wash his robe whereupon the god Sakka provided a wash tank and stone and a nearby

tree bent down its branch for the Buddha to hang his robe on. Another time there was a great rain-storm and the land was inundated. Kassapa went in a boat to see how the Buddha fared and found that he was walking to and fro on firm dry land, untouched by the water. These and other displays of the Buddha's powers finally convinced the hermit brothers and they and their hundreds of followers became the Buddha's disciples.

Now the Buddha remembered his promise to King Bimbisara, namely, that his would be the first kingdom the Buddha would visit after his attainment of Enlightenment. So with a thousand disciples he set out for the city of Rajagaha where he stopped in a grove of palm trees. There, he was visited by King Bimbisara, his court and warriors and a multitude of people who came to pay respect and to hear him preach. In front of this great assembly, the hermit brother Kassapa acknowledged the

Buddha as his teacher and paid reverence to him. And King Bimbisara, having entered the stream that leads to deliverance, at this time gave a bamboo grove called Veluvana to the Buddha for his use as a secluded place to live. There, in the monastery donated by King Bimbisara, the Buddha spent the next three rainy seasons.

Now in the kingdom of Magadha there were two young friends named Upatissa and Kolita, later known as Sariputta and Moggallana. They used to ride on rich, golden palanquins and in horse-drawn carriages until one day they realized the impermanence of things and decided to renounce the world. They studied first under the teacher Sanjaya, and then wandered about in search of a better teacher. After some time, Sariputta, while staying in Rajagaha, met the Buddha's disciple, Assaji – the fifth of the five ascetics converted at the deer park by the Buddha – who uttered to him the stanza beginning: 'Ye dhamma hetuppabhava ... ' (– 'Of things that proceed from a cause, their cause the

Tathagatha has told, and also their cessation, thus teaches the great ascetic'). Recognizing this as the true teaching, Sariputta went to find Moggallana and the two resolved to visit the Buddha at Velu-vana. The Buddha preached to them and ordained them as monks and they became his chief dis-ciples who in time could answer questions within the range of no other disciples of the Buddha. The next rainy season was spent by the Buddha at Vesali where he preached to his monks and to all who came there to see him.

In the sixth year of his ministry the Buddha performed the great miracle of the pairs at Savatthi and defeated sectarian opponents by a display of his superior powers. He next considered what former Buddhas had done and he saw that they had preached the law in Tavatimsa heaven to their mothers. So he raised his right foot and placed it on the top of Yugandhara mountain and his left foot he placed upon Mount Meru and with another stride he reached Tavatimsa heaven and seated himself upon an immense rock (which, called Pandukambala, was the throne of Sakka) under the heavenly

parijata tree. Attended by all the gods of the ten thousand worlds he preached to his mother and ex-
pounded the Abhidhamma. For three months he preached in Tavatimsa heaven. Then on the full
moon day when the Buddha was ready to descend to earth, Sakka prepared a triple stairway, one of
gold for the gods, one of silver for the Brahmas, and a jewelled one in the middle for the Buddha to
descend upon. Accompanied by these deities holding white umbrellas and ceremonial fans, the
Buddha set foot upon the earth at the gateway to the city of Sankassa while all paid reverence to him.

Thus after six rainy seasons had passed the Buddha spent the seventh in Tavatimsa heaven and the eighth preaching in the city of Sumsumaragiri in Bhagga country. The ninth he spent at Ghositarama monastery in Kosambi where he refreshed with the cooling waters of the law five hundred ascetics and others who were ready to receive his teachings. The tenth rainy season he spent in the solitude of the forest of Parileyya where the king of elephants in that country came and ministered to all his needs and paid him very great reverence. The eleventh season was passed in Dakkhinagiri monastery

in a brahmin village called Ekanala where he preached the law to the brahmins of the Bharadvaja clan and others. The Buddha spent the twelfth rainy season in the town of Veranja where, at the end of the season, he and his monk disciples were invited to a meal and presented with offerings by the brahmins of that town. The Buddha, for the remaining years of his long ministry, journeyed throughout northern India, preaching and establishing communities of monks. In particular he spent many rainy seasons at Jetavana monastery in Savatthi with his disciple Ananda his constant attendant.

It was at Jetavana that his disciple, Sariputta, perceiving that in former ages a Buddha's chief disciples had always died first, realised that his own period of life would not extend beyond the next seven days. Sariputta then contemplated in what place he should cease to exist and, seeing that it should be in the house in Nalaka village where he had been born, he requested the Buddha's permission to go there. On his deathbed, Sariputta was visited by the four great guardian gods, by Sakka and by the Brahmas. When his old mother saw this, she perceived the worth of her son and received

from him the Buddha's teaching, and then Sariputta entered into Parinibbana, total escape from the cycle of rebirth and death. His grieving mother ordered five hundred gold shrines and five hundred tiered spires to be made in his honour and built a funeral pyre ninety-nine cubits high. Sariputta's nurse, named Revati, came to offer flowers at the pyre, but was trampled to death in the crush and immediately translated to Tavatimsa heaven from where she descended in a golden ornamented pavilion to pay homage to Sariputta.

After the funeral, Sariputta's relics, his robes and bowl were gathered up by the monk Cunda who took them first to Ananda. Together they went to inform the Buddha who extolled the virtues of Sariputta and caused a shrine enclosing his relics to be built in his memory. Sariputta's death was preceded by that of Rahula who had been ordained by Sariputta at the Buddha's request. The Buddha and his followers then departed for Rajagaha and it was at that time that the Buddha's

disciple Moggallana also attained Parinibbana, as did Kondanna, the brahmin who had foretold that the young Prince Siddhattha would one day become a Buddha. In memory of Moggallana the Buddha also caused a shrine to be built at Jetavana. Rahula's attainment of Parinibbana occurred in Tavatimsa and Kondanna's at the great lake of the Chaddanta elephants.

From Rajagaha the Buddha travelled on to Vesali. There he stopped for a day at the Capala shrine, a pleasant place. Calling Ananda to him, the Buddha praised Vesali and its shrines, adding, 'Ananda, every wise person should be earnest in perfecting himself in the four bases of psychic powers and, if he so chooses, should remain so doing for a whole world cycle. I, the Buddha, having become perfect in these matters, can so remain for as long as I wish'. The Buddha repeated these words three times. But Ananda was deaf to the hint contained therein and, paying reverence, made no answer. Soon after, Mara, the Spirit of Evil, appeared and addressed the Buddha, saying, 'O great Buddha, go now to Nibbana; the time has come'. To which the Buddha replied, 'Do not be concerned, O evil one; very soon, within three months, I shall attain the great Parinibbana'. Upon this utterance of the

Buddha, the earth began to shake violently. Ananda, being afraid, came near to ask the meaning of the earthquake whereupon the Buddha explained the eight causes of the earth so shaking, saying that the seventh cause was, as he had just demonstrated, his mastery and renunciation of existence, and that the eighth cause still to come would be the Buddha's obtaining Parinibbana. Only then did Ananda petition the Buddha thrice over to stay on earth for the benefit of men, gods and Brahmas, during one age of the world. But the Buddha replied, 'Ananda, it is too late, when you remained silent before, to ask this of me now'. The Buddha then told Ananda to assemble all his monks, and he preached, exhorting them to remain faithful to his teachings in order to ensure the continuance of the Sasana, or Buddhist faith.

From Vesali the Buddha, now eighty years of age, continued on his journey to Kusinara, resting along the way in the villages of Bhandagama, Ambagama, Jambugama, Hatthigama and Bhogagama-nagara. On this his final journey, the Buddha preached to his monks on the four bases of mindfulness, that is the four ways of directing the mind to the impurities and impermanence of matter, on the four great authorities, and on the practices which lead to the attainment of Nibbana. At length the Buddha arrived at Pava, a city of the Malla kings. There he stopped at the mango grove which Cunda, the son of a wealthy goldsmith, had presented, with a monastery, to the Buddha. When

Cunda heard that the Buddha had arrived, he was delighted and invited the Buddha and his followers to partake of a meal on the morning of the next day. To the Buddha Cunda served pork and rice, but in accordance with the Buddha's instructions he served other food to his followers. When the Buddha had finished eating, he told Cunda to take what remained of the meal and bury it in a hole in the ground. Soon the Buddha was taken ill, but continued slowly and composedly on his journey to Kusinara. This was his last meal.

On the way to Kusinara, the Buddha became very thirsty and asked Ananda to fetch him water from the river through which the Malla kings had just driven with five hundred ox carts. As the water was so muddied and dirty, Ananda did not want to give it to the Buddha, but the Buddha insisted, asking three times for it, and when Ananda filled the Buddha's bowl the water turned clear and pure. Now Pukkusa, a Malla prince, came and desired to make an offering to the Buddha of two fine robes of the

colour of pure gold. The Buddha accepted one robe and told Pukkusa to give the other to Ananda which would be as if given to all his community of monks (the Sangha) and would be an act of great merit. Ananda in turn then made an offering of this robe to the Buddha who, clothed in them, glittered like a great pillar of fire. And the Buddha told Ananda that his body so glowed because the time had come for him to attain the state of Parinibbana.

The Buddha with his disciples then went down to the bank of the river Kakuttha where he bathed and refreshed himself, and then went into a mango grove, a short distance from the river. There, the Buddha, feeling very fatigued, asked the monk Cunda to double his outer cloth into four folds which he then lay down upon, on his right side. At that moment Ananda arrived and the Buddha, perceiving that the goldsmith's son was troubled of mind because the food he had served had made the Buddha

ill, told him to go to Cunda and to explain to him that there are two offerings of food to a Buddha which are of equal and the greatest merit: the offering of food before the Enlightenment and the offering of the Buddha's very last meal. Cunda's deed was, the Buddha explained, one that would bring him uncommon rewards.

The Buddha then went to the sala grove of the Malla kings on the banks of the Hirannavati river. There he lay down on his right side on a royal couch placed between two trees whose boughs, meeting overhead to form a bower, burst into bloom. All the gods of the ten thousand worlds came and honoured him to the accompaniment of music and dancing. The Buddha then instructed the faithful Ananda on the making of offerings and on what was to be done in the future and preached that good practices and virtuous living were important duties for the continuance of his dispensations. To the assembled monks his last words were: 'Everything is subject to change; strive on without delay'. And so at the dawning of the day the Buddha entered the great Parinibbana. When it was known that the lord Buddha had departed, some monks wailed and lamented, others, possessed of greater

understanding, were calm. Next the Malla kings all came, bringing perfume and fine robes, to mourn and to pay their respects. For seven successive days there was singing and dancing as with music, flowers and perfume they honoured the departed Buddha. On the eighth day the Malla kings put on new robes and bore the body of the Buddha in procession, accompanied by all the gods. Now there was a woman named Mallika, widow of the general Bandhula, who had taken that day a precious gold ornamental cloth and sprinkled it with perfume. Stopping the procession, she spread it like a shroud over the Buddha, praying that she in future births might have no need of ornaments, but might always appear as though ornamented. And, so adorned, the body of the Buddha glowed a beauteous gold.

Outside the eastern gate of the city they built an immense funeral pyre of fragrant sandalwood and, in accordance with Ananda's instructions, the Buddha's body was wrapped five hundred times over in a cotton cloth and then in a fine cloth, and placed in a golden coffin upon the pyre which was one hundred and twenty cubits high. At that time the great Kassapa was on his way from the city of Pava to Kusinara accompanied by five hundred monks when he met an ascetic, bearing aloft like an umbrella an extraordinary mandarava flower. From this flower, which appears only on great and rare occasions associated with Buddhas, Kassapa discerned that the Parinibbana of the Buddha had oc-curred seven days ago. Kassapa, on hearing the monk Subhadda say that they should not grieve, as now they were free of the Buddha's control and could do as they pleased, was shocked and there-

upon resolved to hold an assembly of learned monks to ascertain and preserve correctly the Buddha's teachings. The Malla kings then tried to set fire to the funeral pyre, but the sandalwood would not catch light as the gods were waiting for Kassapa to arrive to pay reverence to the Buddha's body. Kassapa, hands raised to his forehead, circled the pyre three times and then, where he stopped, the sacred feet of the Buddha appeared from the coffin – whereupon Kassapa bowed his head beneath them and all paid reverence. Only then, and without the aid of men or gods, did the funeral pyre catch fire and all was consumed, apart from various sacred relics. After this, streams of water came down from the sky between the two sala trees and the Malla kings also poured scented water to extinguish the fire.

When the fire was extinguished, the Malla kings put the relics in a gold receptacle and placed them under a white umbrella on the back of a splendidly caparisoned elephant. Offerings of flowers were presented and the relics were taken to the city in a grand procession of elephants, horses, chariots and soldiers, all in close formation. For seven days the sacred relics were guarded there in a special

pavilion, with white umbrellas placed over them, so that all from near and far might have an opportunity to come and pay reverence to the relics. And the Malla kings and princes were at first disposed to keep for themselves these sacred relics of the Buddha. Soon King Ajatasattu, son of King Bimbisara, and kings in other kingdoms heard of the demise of the Buddha.

These kings all sent messages and then came to ask the Malla kings for the Buddha's relics, that they might build a shrine over them, make offerings and reverence them. It seemed that the kings were even ready to go to war for possession of the relics. At this point, a brahmin named Dona intervened and appeased the kings, reminding them that the Buddha had preached forbearance in all matters, and proposing an equal division of the relics into eight portions. This proposal was accepted. While distributing the relics Dona secreted one – the right eye-tooth – on his person, but Sakka perceived this and carried off the relic to Tavatimsa heaven where he placed it in the Culamani shrine. Then

King Ajatasattu caused a road to be made to his palace and the relics were borne in a golden receptacle before a great assembly of people and gods for seven days until the city of Rajagaha was reached. And the other kings similarly bore home the relics with honour and built pagodas enshrining the sacred relics of the Buddha in their kingdoms. Now Kassapa took steps to ensure the relics would endure and predicted that in times to come a great emperor named Asoka would find the relics and cause them and the Buddha's teaching to spread from the Buddha's homeland to many other lands. And so indeed in the fullness of time it came to pass.

# *Appendix*

The following notes are designed to help readers identify and examine more closely the episodes from the Buddha's life, as related and depicted in the book. They include comments on both the Buddhist context and the paintings. Artistic features are described first, followed, where necessary, by an explanation of textual terms. The English text of the main picture sequence is based on the Burmese text of the Burney manuscripts, supplemented by reference to the full version of the *Mala lingara wuthtu*.

Each double opening from the original Burmese manuscripts reproduced in this book is, for the purposes of identification in the notes, divided into four 'sides' representing the folds of the original concertina format manuscript which can be seen faintly as a vertical line through the middle of each printed page. In the notes below, these sides are referred to (from left to right) as 'a', 'b', 'c', and 'd'. Various artistic conventions (the gilding of the figure of the Buddha, for example) and general stylistic features are described in the Introduction. The folio numbers of the manuscripts are given first, followed by the page numbers on which they are reproduced in this book.

## OR. 14297
### f.2-3 (p.20-21)
### The Bodhisatta as Sumedha

(a) The king, seated in his palace under a tiered roof spire (Burmese, *pyatthat*) gives orders to his ministers for a feast to be prepared in honour of Dipankara Buddha. On either side of the king are two white umbrellas on stands. These form part of the Burmese royal regalia – only the Buddha and royalty are entitled to a white umbrella. The king wears his ceremonial robes (those of the god Sakka), appropriate for an encounter with a Buddha. The ministers, kneeling before him, wear the long draped velvet robes and tall hats of high-ranking Burmese officials.

(b) The gilded figure of the hermit Sumedha who, exercising his yogic powers, hovers in the air and witnesses the preparations for the feast.

(b-c, centre) Men and women clearing and preparing the road for Dipankara. The workmen are painted with slightly coarse faces and hair, and work bare-chested with their lower garment looped up between their legs, while a foreman, seated (c, foreground), directs operations. The city gateway has a plain three-tiered roof.

(c-d, upper) Dipankara, followed by yellow-robed monks, each carrying an alms bowl, enters through a two-tiered gateway and, hand uplifted, proclaims that Sumedha (the gilded figure prostrated at his feet) will one day also become a Buddha. Kneeling on Sumedha's left and holding lotus flowers is a girl who was, in his final existence, to become his wife Yasodhara.

The historical Buddha, Gotama, is believed by Buddhists to have been preceded by many other Buddhas over a period of incalculable aeons. The world, according to Buddhist thought, exists over an infinite number of immense time spans or world cycles (called *kappa* in Pali; *kalpa* in Sanskrit) which in turn each has other time divisions and during which successive Buddhas have manifested themselves. In the present era (known as *bhaddakappa*) four Buddhas, of whom Gotama is the last, have appeared and there remains one (Metteyya, the future Buddha; Maitreya in Sanskrit) yet to come. Of the previous Buddhas, the names of 27 others (besides Gotama) are known and Dipankara was the very first of the 24 Buddhas who immediately preceded Gotama. It was in Dipankara's lifetime that the hermit Sumedha received the first prophetic intimation that he himself would become a Buddha (i.e., Gotama).

The Bodhisatta (Buddha-to-be) over an immense period of many previous existences had to perfect himself to become a Buddha, acquiring the Ten Perfections (Pali, *dasa parami*) or principal virtues which are: the perfect exercise of generosity (*dana*), morality (*sila*), renunciation (*nekkhama*), wisdom (*panna*), diligence (*viriya*), patience (*khanti*), truth (*sacca*), resolution (*adhitthana*), loving kindness (*metta*) and equanimity (*upekkha*). Each of these is subdivided into the ordinary, the inferior and the unlimited perfection of the virtue, so making thirty in

*Left* Painted back cover of Or. 14298.

all. Each virtue is achieved by a Bodhisatta in all three degrees. The Five Great Charities or Renunciations (*panca mahapariccaga*) are the sacrifice of the most valuable of treasures: kingdom/possessions, children, wife, any limb or feature, and body and life (a variant listing is: children, wife, goods, life, one's self). The Three Good Works (*cariya*) consist of perfect conduct to all sentient beings, to one's family and friends, and to oneself with the object of becoming a Buddha.

## f.4-5 (p.22-23)
### The last rebirths

(a) Scenes from the Vessantara Jataka. The upper scene shows Prince Vessantara in hermit robes and hat seated in his forest abode with, behind him, his two children. He pours water over the hands of the white-robed brahmin Jujaka to seal the gift of his children to Jujaka. The lower scene depicts (right) Vessantara's wife kept at bay in the forest by wild beasts (a tiger, leopard and a Burmese *chin-the* or griffin-lion) so that she will not witness Vessantara giving away her children and Jujaka (extreme left) leading them off.

(b) Reborn in Tusita heaven as Setaketu, the Bodhisatta is shown, flanked by gods and seated on his throne with above, in a circle, (left) a hare and (right) a peacock. These symbolize the moon and sun, and represent the ancient lunar and solar lineages to which Burmese kings laid claim and also sought to associate themselves with the Buddha's Sakya lineage. These symbols also appeared on the thrones of the Burmese kings. According to Buddhist cosmography, the mansions/chariots of the sun and moon are situated half-way up the cosmic axis, Mount Meru. Below the throne in tiers are depicted, rather roughly, five ranks of supernatural creatures who are attendants of the four guardian gods and protect Mount Meru (see below).

(c-d) The four great guardian gods, holding two-edged swords, guard Queen Mahamaya after she has conceived the Buddha-to-be. This kind of sword (called *than-lyet* in Burmese) is also an emblem of Burmese royalty, and only the king was permitted such a sword. It is an essential component of the Burmese coronation regalia. The king is shown seated beyond her and above him rise the tiered gilded spires that mark the centre of the palace and symbolize the centre of the universe, replicating the heavenly mansions of the gods. In Buddhist art, the conception is usually represented as a white elephant who came to the queen in a dream and entered her

side, but the artist has chosen not to depict this.

The Jataka (literally 'birth tales') or stories of the Buddha's previous existences are full of examples of the Buddha's exercise of the Ten Perfections and other moral virtues. The Pali Buddhist canon and the later commentary (*Jatakatthakatha*) contain 547 such stories (which are, however, referred to by the Burmese as 550) of which the last ten or great Jataka are the most well known and popular. The Vessantara Jataka is the very last Jataka and tells of the Buddha's existence as Prince Vessantara who was banished to the forest for giving away the kingdom's sacred white elephant. While living there as a hermit, Vessantara was visited by an old brahmin called Jujaka who came, at the urging of his nagging young wife, to ask for his children as servants. To prevent Vessantara's wife, Maddi, from seeing the children given away, the gods in the form of wild beasts detained her in the forest. Later, Vessantara also gave away Maddi (to the god Sakka in disguise). After many travails, all are reunited. The Vessantara Jataka is a favourite subject for illustration in Burmese art.

Tusita heaven is the fourth of the six lower heavenly worlds of the gods (in Pali, *deva*, meaning 'radiant beings', but often simply called *nat* in the Burney text) and it is where the Bodhisatta awaits his last rebirth. There the gods of the 10,000 worlds assemble to request the Bodhisatta to be born among men. Burmese Buddhist cosmology is complex and, although derived from ancient Indian cosmology, differs in various respects and regards the gods as subject to rebirth and serving the Buddha. Gotama Buddha did not expound any cosmological theories and the essence of his teaching is unaffected by such matters. The universe is divided into three spheres (*dhatu*) – also known as planes (*bhumi*) or worlds (*loka*). These are the world of desire or the sensual sphere (*kamaloka*, or *kamadhatu*), the world of form (*rupaloka*) and the world of formlessness (*arupaloka*). The lowest is the sensual world of desire which ranges from layers of hells through the realms of animals, ghosts (*peta*), and demons (*asurakaya* – often also classed as fallen gods called *asura* who, according to Burmese cosmology, live in three great ruby carbuncular rocks beneath the cosmic mountain), and human beings on to the heavens of the gods (*deva*) at the highest point of the sensual world. Halfway up the cosmic mountain Mount Meru (Pali, *Sumeru* or *Sineru*, *Myin-mo* in Burmese) is the lowest of the *deva* worlds, called *Catummaharajika*, the abode of the four guardian gods or regent kings (Pali, *Cattaro Maharajano*;

*Satumaharit Nat Min-gyi* in Burmese) who guard the four quarters of the world (and are sometimes also referred to as *lokapala*). They undertake the protection of future Buddhas from the moment of their conception (as in the scene depicted). The guardian gods have retinues of celestial musicians (*gandhabba*), monsters (*kumbhanda*), various spirits (*yakkha*) including ogres or *balu* in Burmese, serpents (*naga*), and great mythical birds (usually known by their Sanskrit name, *garuda*; or in Pali, *garula* and in Burmese, *galon*; also sometimes called *supanna*). These are depicted on the pillar supporting the throne in Tusita heaven.

The four guardian gods report to the god Sakka (known as Thagya-min in Burmese; the Vedic god Indra) who reigns over Tavatimsa, heaven of the 33 gods, at the top of Mount Meru. Sakka is the guardian of moral law in the world and plays an important part in Buddhist cosmology, aiding the Bodhisatta in many of his existences. Above this comes Yama heaven, the abode of a class of *deva* called Yama, then Tusita heaven, and then Nimmanarati and Paranimmita-vasavatti, the two highest heavens of the sense-desire world. After this comes the world of form divided into many levels of heavens where live a higher order of gods called Brahma, and above that the world of formlessness. Surrounding Mount Meru are seven rings of mountains with seven seas and beyond, in the great ocean plane bounded by the walls of the universe (*cakkavala*), are four great island continents of which the southern, called Jambudipa (rose-apple island) is the abode of man. Only in Jambudipa are Buddhas born to teach the law of deliverance from the round of rebirth into any level of the three realms of formlessness, form and sense-desire.

## f.6-7 (p.24-25)
## Prince Siddhattha's birth and the brahmins' prophecy

(a, upper) Queen Mahamaya, attended by women in a curtained enclosure, stands holding a branch of the flowering sala tree. The queen's left hand is draped around the shoulder of a kneeling woman who holds the queen's waist. She is traditionally held to be the queen's sister, Pajapati, who becomes the Bodhisatta's foster mother when the queen dies seven days after the baby's birth. Another attendant clasps her round the legs.

(b, upper) Outside the enclosure in front of a woven screen background, the baby (depicted like a small golden Buddha image) is passed from the hands of

Brahmas to the guardian gods and from them to men. The Buddha-to-be is thus ministered to by three levels of beings. When taking his first seven steps, he is shown full size in white robes with a white umbrella held over him, with four gods making obeisance and two more (above) coming down to do the same.

(a-b, lower) The procession and palanquin bearing Queen Mahamaya on her way to (and from) Lumbini grove. Two white umbrellas are held aloft the tiered roofs of the palanquin in the procession which is headed by guards and the royal ministers. The palanquin, or litter, is commented on by Burney in his notes as being 'such as is now in use by the King and Queen of Ava'.

(c) The infant is presented by the king to the brown-robed sage Kaladevala who is depicted twice, once smiling and (behind) weeping, as he realizes he will not live to see the child attain Enlightenment. The infant's placing its feet upon the head of the sage indicates its superiority as it is a mark of respect to place one's head at the feet of one's superior.

(d) The eight white-robed brahmins make their prophecies, each holding up two fingers, except for the youngest brahmin, Kondanna, at the rear. At the Burmese court it was customary for brahmin astrologers to examine a child's hand and predict its future.

## f.8-9 (p.26-27)
## The ploughing ceremony and the Prince's marriage

(a, upper) King Suddhodana, in gilded martial dress and helmet and bearing the double-edged sword, rides forth on his handsomely caparisoned elephant to perform the annual ploughing ceremony to ensure the fertility of the kingdom's crops. Charmingly, he is depicted carrying his young son (gilded) on the white elephant, with a white umbrella aloft. The white elephant is especially significant and revered as representing the Buddha's conception and previous incarnation, and possession of one was highly prized by Burmese and Thai monarchs.

(a, lower) The Bodhisatta, seated crosslegged in meditation, is depicted in a low railed gilded seat that in part resembles an old style swinging cradle, with a cloth canopy, under a tree where he is reverenced by his father.

(b, upper) Prince Siddhattha, holding a black *parabaik* (folding book) faces his tutor whose wife kneels behind, with banana trees in fruit and bud in the background.

(b, lower) The ploughing ceremony. The king's plough and the yoke and horns of the bullocks drawing it are gilded.

(c-d, upper) The Prince, as befits a scion of the warrior class, displays his skills in archery, using a gilded naga-headed bow. The elephants lined up to attend the display of martial arts are, together with the king's elephant (a), depicted in a most accomplished manner. The stippling of the face, trunk and ears of the grey elephants is characteristic of most Burmese elephant paintings.

(c-d, lower) The Prince and his bride, wearing a high-crowned headdress, join hands in marriage. Behind them on an inner (eastern) door post, hang green coconuts and bananas which are offerings to the spirits (known as *nat* in Burmese). Celebrations include a dancer, dramatic performance and a group of musicians. The dancer is shown under a white-roofed dome supported by thin pillars. This appears to be the 'umbrella room' – a structure (usually with a central supporting pillar) in the palace grounds where dramatic performances took place at the Burmese court. The man wearing a horse's head prances in the manner of a horse while just visible on the 'rider' behind are, on his waist and knees, black tattoos. The musical instruments consist of a 16 gong circle (*kyi-waing*), a drum circle (*pat-waing*), a large cylindrical drum (*pat-ma*), a flute (*hne*) and cymbals (*lagwin*).

Henry Burney, in his notes, comments upon the royal ploughing ceremony that 'Mr Lane once saw this ceremony at Ava, and he informs me that the king used a plough like that in the picture, and that not only the king, but all the princes and principal officers performed the ceremony of standing upon the plough for a short distance'. Charles Lane was an English merchant and long term resident at the Burmese capital who was on good terms with the king and court.

The young Bodhisatta is said to have concentrated on the flow of breath in and out (*anapana kammathanam*) and to have reached straight away the first of the five states of mind (*jhana*) in meditation.

## f.10-11 (p.28-29)
### The Four Omens and the Renunciation

(a) The Prince presents his pearl necklace to the maiden who has greeted him on his return from seeing the four signs or omens. A whole fold having been devoted to this scene, the rest of the opening is compositionally crowded, and the events are not shown in order of their occurrence.

(b-c, centre) The Prince draws back a curtain and bids a silent farewell to his wife, sleeping with her hand resting on her baby son, with the palace dancers and musicians asleep in ungainly postures in the foreground and his attendant and horse (with gilded saddle) awaiting him outside the chamber. The curtains are of unusual patterns. In front of the palace ladies is a gilded curved Burmese harp on a stand (the painter has omitted the strings).

(b-c, lower) The Prince out riding in his gilded carriage (depicted with a tiered roof) sees and points to the four omens: an old man, a sick man, a corpse (being pecked at by a bird) and a holy man or monk, carrying the customary circular fan.

(d, lower) The Prince, seated in the gardens on a propitious stone slab reserved for royalty, and decked with royal ornaments sent by Sakka through the god Vissakamma in the guise of a valet, receives the news of the birth of his son. In the foreground is a royal bathing tank in which, in some manuscripts, the prince is depicted bathing before donning his ornaments.

(d, upper) The Prince, painted against a flower-spangled red background, and wearing white and gold robes, rides out of the palace through a two-tiered gateway, with the gods in attendance. In many other manuscript representations of this scene (see, for comparison, the illustrations on p.16-17 of the Introduction), the gods are shown holding the hooves of the horse in their hands to muffle the sound, but here they are only shown holding lights. Mara, holding up one hand and with a sword in the other, stands barring his way. In other manuscripts Mara is depicted with a dark green or blue skin and looking more malevolent. The flowered background represents the fabulous flowers that filled the sky and showered down to earth at the time of the Bodhisatta's departure or great renunciation.

Some texts refer to the prince making four outings in his carriage, encountering each sign or omen on a separate occasion. It had been predicted at Prince Siddhattha's birth that if he saw these four signs he would resolve to renounce the world. The signs are important subjects for Buddhist meditation on the suffering or kinds of misery that all beings are liable to. On learning of the birth of his son, the prince is said to have stated: 'An impediment (*rahula*) has come into being; a bond has arisen' and it is for this reason that the child was named Rahula. Kisagotami's joyful words (a famous Pali verse beginning '*nibbuta nana sa mata ...*') brought to the prince's mind, agitated by the four omens, the pleasant intelligence of Nibbana.

Mara (called by the Burmese Man Nat) is the powerful Spirit of Evil or God of Death who resides in (or on the fringes of) the highest heaven (Paranimitta-vasavatti) of the sensual world and seeks dominion over all the lower parts of the universe. He opposes anyone aspiring to attain the state of Enlightenment and his challenges and temptations to the Buddha symbolize the struggle between good and evil.

## f.11b-13a (p.30-31)
### The Prince's tonsure and enrobing

(a) Described under (d) above.

(b, upper) The Prince, depicted now in gilded robes, leaps the river Anoma on his horse. The water is, in typical Burmese style, depicted with overlapping hoops of waves out of which peep fish and other creatures.

(c, upper) The Prince, seated, cuts off his long hair which is caught in the air by Sakka, while (foreground) the eight requisites of a monk are presented to him by a god holding a gilded casket and another offering the round alms bowl. The gilded flowers topping the casket resemble the mythical padesa tree (Burmese, *padetha bin*) which is unique to the northern island and produces whatever an applicant desires; but they must represent the lotus flowers that, according to tradition, sprang up at the centre of Jambudipa, and correspond to the number of Buddhas that will appear in that world cycle; within each lotus flower is said to be a complete set of monk's requisites (*attha parikkhara*) that are taken and looked after by the Brahmas until needed. Burney in his notes simply comments that '... over the priest's clothes which are being presented, a bouquet of flowers is placed as an ornament according to the custom in Ava when anything is presented particularly to the priests or images'.

(b-c, lower) Prince Siddhattha's attendant, Channa, and horse are instructed to return to the palace. When the horse dies of grief (b, bottom scene) Channa, crying, is left to return on foot, carrying the saddle.

(d) Now robed as a monk and with his alms bowl slung from his shoulder, the Buddha-to-be begins his quest for Enlightenment. His robes are from this point on gilded, but his bowl (unlike in some other manuscripts) is not and matches other monks' bowls. The usual rounded cranial protusion (*usnisa*) of the

Buddha is depicted with a slight depression where his topknot of hair has been cut off.

## f.13b-15a (p.32-33)
### King Bimbisara meets the Bodhisatta

(a) The Bodhisatta (upper) enters the city of Rajagaha and (lower) receives alms in his bowl.

(b) King Bimbisara, holding the royal yaktail fan-whisk, and seated in his palace, is told of the Bodhisatta's arrival.

(c-d, lower) King Bimbisara, now wearing royal white robes (the costume of the god Sakka), rides forth from his palace. Behind him are four ministers bearing white umbrellas and royal regalia betel boxes.

(c-d, upper) Against a background of a rock cave, the Bodhisatta partakes of his meal, while Bimbisara pays reverence.

Bimbisara was king of Magadha and reigned in the city of Rajagaha for 52 years. He was an early and noted patron of the Buddha.

## f.15-16 (p.34-35)
### Austerities and Sujata's offering

(a) The rocky cave forms a background for the scene described above and for that of the Buddha's austerities as a wandering monk (see b, upper).

(b, lower) The Bodhisatta with his first teachers, Alara and Uddaka.

(b, upper) The Bodhisatta, weakened by prolonged fasting, lies on his right side with (foreground) his five companions in attendance. He is not here shown as an emaciated figure, this being a representation which is more common in Indian Buddhist art than in Burmese art.

(c, upper) The house and family of Sujata. Her father is smoking a long-stemmed pipe. The wooden house, raised on stilts, and with a balcony is typical of a Burmese village house of some substance.

(c, lower) Sujata preparing her offering in a large cooking pot over a fire, tended by the gods.

(d, lower) Sujata and her maid on their way to make the offering in a gold bowl and the Bodhisatta receiving the offering.

The Bodhisatta practised austerities (*dukkha-cariya*) for six years and found it was like a time of trying to tie knots in the air. From Alara he learnt how to attain the advanced state of concentration known as the realm of nothingness (*akincannayatana*) and from Uddaka the stage known as the realm of neither perception nor non-perception (*neva sanna nasannyatana*), but realizing that the highest truth has to be found within oneself, he ceased to seek other teachers. His five companions (*pancavaggiya*) were Kondanna, the young brahmin soothsayer who had foretold he would become a Buddha, and four sons of the other court brahmins who had retired to the forest in anticipation of his Enlightenment.

The offering prepared by Sujata was made, the texts explain, from special, extremely concentrated milk obtained by giving the milk of 1,000 cows to 500 cows, then their milk to 250, and so on, until reduced down to the milk of eight cows.

## f.17-18 (p.36-37)
### The Naga King and Sotthiya

(a) The Bodhisatta (upper) eats Sujata's offering and (lower) casts the golden bowl into the river where it floats upstream.

(a-b) The Naga King is shown in his palace with the bowls of the three previous Buddhas of this era stacked beside him. In the water frolic winged elephants and horses.

(c) The grass cutter presents the Bodhisatta with handfuls of grass (lower scene) which turn into a throne (upper).

(d) Seated crosslegged on the throne, the Bodhisatta begins his meditation. Among the attendant gods present are Brahma holding the white umbrella, Sakka holding his conch-shell (*vijayuttara-sankha*) which is blown at the moment of Enlightenment, Pancasikha who plays the harp (and in Buddhist cosmology carries reports from the four guardian gods to Sakka's charioteer, Matali), and Santusita king of Tusita heaven, holding the fan-whisk. The Bodhisatta is depicted from this point on in the manuscript with a gilded flame finial.

Mahakala, the Naga King (also called Kalanaga) resides in the world under the river Neranjara and – his life span being one *kappa* – saw all four Buddhas of this era.

## f.19-20 (p.38-39)
### Mara's attack and the Enlightenment

(a-c) This dramatic scene, painted against a rich red backdrop, depicts the assault of Mara's army upon the Buddha as he meditates. Mara atop a gilded elephant's howdah is shown first (on the left) with a yellowy-green face like a demon's, and with ten arms, wielding nine weapons. The faces of Mara's warriors are coarse and fierce; some have tattooed thighs.

(b) Beneath the Buddha on his throne at the foot of the Bodhi tree is the figure of the earth goddess who bears witness to the Buddha's previous good deeds by wringing out her long hair, so releasing the water absorbed into the earth when water is ceremonially poured when making gifts and acts of merit.

(c) The water sweeps away Mara's warriors who are shown in flight and disarray with their pennants and lances broken. Some are being devoured by the animals which had been their mounts, while two figures (one, green-faced, on an elephant's back is presumably Mara although not matching the first figure of Mara) look back and join hands in reverence to the Buddha. The flowers scattered against the red background represent the army's weapons which, when discharged, fell harmlessly to earth as flowers. In most representations of this event the Buddha is shown in the earth-touching gesture, but unusually in this manuscript he is depicted in this scene with both hands extended and only in the next scene (d) with his right hand touching the ground.

(d) The Buddha, at the moment of his Enlightenment, is represented with a halo, or nimbus round his head, from which issue streams of different coloured lights. Kneeling at the base of the throne are depicted the greater and lesser gods who had all fled at the onslaught of Mara's army.

The early Pali texts do not mention the earth goddess (known as Wathondaye in Burmese), and the story of her appearance at this time is a popular Southeast Asian interpolation, found in the *Pathama-sambodhi* text. Burmese renditions of this scene may reflect Thai artistic influence, although in Thai versions the earth goddess is depicted standing and the army advancing from the other side. In Indian and Sinhalese depictions of this temptation scene, the earth goddess is sometimes shown carrying a vase as she emerges from the earth in response to his call, but the episode of the washing away of Mara's army in the water released from her hair is not known or depicted. Gotama's victory over Mara is considered as one of his 'eight great victories' and Burney comments in his notes: 'Brahmins apply these eight victories to the Kings of Ava on days of ceremony when they recite prayers at the foot of the throne'. Among the other victories are the Buddha's taming of the mad Nalagiri elephant, his conversion of the thief Angulimala and of the monster Alavaka.

The stages of meditation by which the Buddha gained insight into perfect knowledge and attained Enlightenment are complex and outside the scope of this study. Among his attainments were knowledge of one's and others' former states of existence (*pubbenivasanussati-nana*) which is one of the faculties of an arahat, superhuman vision (*dibba-cakkhu*), possession of the ten strengths (*dasa bala*) which are of two kinds: power of the mind and power of the body, realization of the four noble truths and of the law of dependent origination (*paticca-samuppada*). The place where he attained Enlightenment is now called Buddha Gaya (or Bodh Gaya).

## f.21-22 (p.40-41)
### The seven stations: weeks 1-4

(a) The first week, seated in meditation on the throne.

(b) The second week. The Buddha, with a flaming nimbus and his feet circled by lotuses, contemplates the seat of his Enlightenment. The base of the throne has changed in appearance.

(c) The third week with the Buddha shown in a railed gilded enclosure (his walkway).

(d) The fourth week with the Buddha seated in a gilded house. This whole opening is richly gilded with a spacious and quite large scale composition, each scene divided by flowering branches and trees and linked by a foreground filled with smiling bullocks, frolicking rabbits and happy goats.

## f.23-24 (p.42-43)
### The seven stations: weeks 5-7

(a) The fifth week when the Buddha, seated on his throne in earth-touching gesture, is visited by a bearded, white-robed brahmin (left) and by the three daughters of Mara as young women (right), and as bent old women (below).

(b) The Buddha sheltered by the great Mucalinda Naga during the sixth week. The white-robed figure (left, foreground) is either Mara, or (more in accord with the full *Mala lingara* text) the Naga, now transformed into a young man who pays homage to the Buddha.

(c) At the end of the seventh week, the Buddha is presented with gifts by Sakka (right), unusually shown in coloured robes, while the four guardian gods (left) present four bowls which (centre) become a single bowl with four gilded rims.

(d) The two merchant brothers kneel with their solid wheeled, covered bullock carts in the foreground while the bullocks rest under trees.

The compass directions of each of the seven sites or

stations (*sattatthana*) of the Buddha in relation to the Bodhi tree have been the subject of scholarly debate as texts and representations in art are not consistent. The shortened Burney text under these scenes only mentions a direction for the seventh week, but the full *Mala lingara* text gives more details. The Buddha's throne changes in appearance from scene to scene in the Burney *parabaik* sequence. Mara's daughters bore the names Tanha ('desire'), Arati ('aversion') and Raga ('lust'). According to some versions, Mara petitions the Buddha to restore his daughters to their former youth and beauty – the same accounts having inappropriately asserted that the Buddha had changed them into an undesirable form.

Some Burmese texts omit Sakka's gift of a toothstick, and the source of the water (Anotatta lake); the myrobalan fruit has medicinal, cleansing properties.

The merchant brothers are said in the Burney text to have come from Ramanna(-desa) which means Lower Burma, and although the Burney text does not mention the Buddha's gift to them of some hairs from his head, the full *Mala lingara* text does, based on old Mon and early Burmese foundation legends of the Shwe Dagon pagoda that hold that the sacred hair relics were brought to Burma by the merchant brothers and enshrined there.

## f.25-26 (p.44-45)
### The first sermon

(a) While at the foot of the Ajapala tree (to which he had returned), the Buddha is petitioned by the gods to preach to mankind.

(b) The Buddha (upper) encounters Upaka and (lower) his five former companions.

(c) Seated on a rounded lotus throne, with a large nimbus of streaming light, the Buddha delivers his first sermon in the deer park (with three deer in the foreground) to the five ascetics (left) and gods (right). The Buddha is not represented in the preaching gesture.

(d) Yasa, the first lay convert, is shown (upper) in a scene that echoes Prince Siddhattha's disgust at the worldly pleasures of palace life, and (below) setting out to find the Buddha. The care with which Yasa is painted and the splendour of his costume may indicate that the commissioner/donor of the manuscript is here portrayed.

The *Dhammacakkappavattana* sutta contains the essence of the Buddha's message of the path to salvation. The five wandering ascetics, on hearing it, become 'stream entrants' (Pali, *sotapanna*) or 'established in the fruit of the steam-entrant stage' and on the path to arahatship and Nibbana. This reception of the Buddha's teaching sets a key pattern whereby those who hear his preaching are said to 'enter the stream', some at different stages according to their individual understanding and attainments. The stages, and resultant levels of rebirth, are: stream-entrant (*sotapanna*) – sometimes translated as 'convert' – who will not be reborn in hell, as an animal or a ghost; once-returner (*sakadagami*) who will only have one more human rebirth; non-returner (*anagami*) who will be reborn in a higher world and attain Nibbana there; and a perfected or worthy being (*arahat*), one in whom the five aggregates or elements of being (*khanda*) have been eliminated, that is who has attained Nibbana in this life and will never be reborn in any form. The Buddha's first disciples became arahats (in Burmese, *yahanda*) at the conclusion of the Buddha's sermon on the characteristics of non-self (*Anattalakkhana sutta*) preached five days after his first sermon.

Upaka, encountered by the Buddha on his way to the deer park, represents an individual who was not at first willing to listen to the Buddha (although later he did enter the right path). The place where the Buddha preached his first sermon is today known as Sarnath.

## f.27-28 (p.46-47)
### The first disciples

(a) Yasa, now robed as a monk, kneels before the Buddha. Yasa's old father (right, foreground) has come in search of his son.

(b) The family and household of Yasa reverence the Buddha, in a curtained enclosure, to whom they have offered food.

(c) Kneeling before the Buddha are Yasa's family, friends and other followers. In the foreground stand Yasa and his four friends, all in monks' robes and carrying their alms bowls.

(d) The monks, who have now all attained arahatship, disperse to spread the Buddha's teaching.

## f.29b-31a (p.48-49)
### Conversion of the hermit brothers

(a) The Buddha, feet in a circle of lotuses, meets the elder hermit brother who carries a curly poker stick and points to his dwelling.

(b-c) The hermits' residence is depicted as a solid two storey structure. The Buddha, seated in the wooden

roofed and railed outside kitchen extension, pays no attention to the Naga beside him.

(d) The Naga, tamed, is displayed in the Buddha's bowl while the hermits both marvel and shrink in fear.

## f.32-33 (p.50-51)
### Further miraculous displays

(a) Kassapa invites the Buddha to a meal.

(b) The Buddha holds out to Kassapa the *jambu* fruit.

(c-d) The Buddha, depicted with a large, flaming nimbus, walks on dry land while hermits struggle in the water.

(d, upper) Sakka holds the branch of a tree for the Buddha to hang his washed robe upon. At his feet is the flat washing stone.

The Kassapa brothers were fire worshippers, and to them the Buddha delivered his famous Fire Sermon (*Adittapariyaya sutta*) which states that all man's existence is burning with the fires of lust, hate and delusion. (This discourse was the source for section III of T. S. Eliot's '*The Waste Land*'). The Indian context of fire worship and sacrifice has been transmuted in the Burmese text, so that the room where the Buddha spends the night is the hermits' 'cook-house' rather than fire or altar chamber. The Burney manuscript devotes much space to illustrating the different ways in which the Buddha convinced the Kassapa brothers of his superior powers. Other incidents from the Burney *parabaik* not reproduced in this book are the Buddha splitting wood and making it kindle which the hermits had not been able to do, his creation of 500 braziers of fire to warm them after bathing, and the hermits casting their utensils (curly, pronged poker sticks and axes) and vessels into the water and submitting to the Buddha. The hermits were 'matted-haired' and their hair is depicted sometimes in a conical peak; their brown robes consist of two pieces of cloth and are not the same as Buddhist monks' three-piece robes (*ticivara*). The brothers' names were Uruvela-Kassapa, Nadi-Kassapa and Gaya-Kassapa. The elder brother, after he became the Buddha's disciple, is often referred to as Mahakassapa.

## f.37-38 (p.52-53)
### The visit to King Bimbisara's kingdom

(a) The Buddha and monks in the palm tree grove. The leaves and palm nuts are carefully and naturalistically painted.

(b, upper) The yellow-robed monk hovering in the air between the clumps of palm trees is Kassapa who, according to some texts, rose into the air seven times to demonstrate his powers and his submission to the Buddha's far superior powers and teaching.

(b-d) King Bimbisara (lower left), in white and gold robes, kneels at the head of his procession of ministers and soldiers (carrying long-barrelled guns and spears and painted with a variety of skin colours and expressions). Conspicuously and unreverentially upright are depicted (d, lower) two Westerners, with brown curly hair, wearing hats with upturned brims, buttoned undershirts and heavy, wide-cuffed dress coats, striped trousers, and – another mark of disrespect – shoes (with upturned toes), and carrying over their shoulders ramrods or tapers for the cannon. They stand in front of two gilded gun carriages and exemplify the Burmese artists' habit of incorporating contemporary features into their paintings – in this case foreign mercenaries (or descendants thereof) who were often employed/captured by the Burmese kings for their knowledge of guns and metalcasting. Also standing, in front of the foreigners and holding the reins of a horse, is a moustachioed man with tattooed knees and shoulders, while another tattooed man kneels in front of the horse. As was customary in old Burma, the tattoos (to convey invulnerability and also, in the case of soldiers, for identification) on the upper half of the body are in red, while those from just above the waist to just below the knees are in black or indigo.

## f.40-41 (p.54-55)
### Sariputta and Moggallana

(a-b) The Buddha seated with his disciples in the bamboo grove donated by King Bimbisara.

(c) Sariputta (lower) in a litter and Moggallana (upper) in a one-horse carriage; both are richly dressed, with umbrellas held aloft, in the style of royal ministers.

(d) The Buddha (unusally shown ungilded - an artistic oversight?) at Vesali.

The stanza recited to Sariputta and Moggallana by Assaji skilfully and succinctly expresses the essentials of the Buddha's teaching of the law of cause and effect. The Pali text is: '*Ye dhamma hetuppabhava tesam hetum tathagatho aha tesan ca yo nirodha, evam vadi mahasamano*'. Often referred to as the 'Buddhist creed', these lines are found inscribed on many votive plaques and images. After the

conversion of Sariputta and Moggallana, the *Mala lingara* narrates many incidents which are often illustrated in other Burmese life of the Buddha manuscripts, but are omitted from the Burney manuscripts. Among these are the Buddha's visit to his native Kapilavatthu and the conversion of his father King Suddhodana and other family members, and the entry into the monkhood of the Buddha's (half-) brother, Nanda, and of his own young son Rahula. Their ordination left King Suddhodana without an heir and, seeking to spare other parents similar distress, he requested that in future no child should be ordained with parental consent. Also said to have been ordained at this time was the Buddha's cousin, Ananda, who became his constant companion and, during the Buddha's 20th rainy season, was appointed his chief attendant. It was Ananda who persuaded the Buddha to establish an order of nuns and allow Queen Pajapati, after the death of King Suddhodana, to become a nun. Also omitted from the Burney manuscripts is the story of Jivaka the physician and a long sequence about how the Buddha forbade his disciples to display their powers and announced that he would instead display his own great powers at Savatthi at the foot of a mango tree. (For details and illustrations of some of these scenes in other Burmese manuscripts, see the Introduction). It was after this that the Buddha ascended into the sky and performed the 'twin miracle' (*yamaka patihariya*) of fire and water – a phenomenon whereby fire and water streamed from the Buddha's body – and then, in three strides, reached Tavatimsa. The twin miracle which really defies successful artistic representation is included in the Burney *parabaik*, but is not here reproduced.

## f.43-44 (p.56-57)
### The descent from Tavatimsa heaven

(a-b) The Buddha, painted with gilded body and reddish-orange robes, stands (left) on Yugandhara (represented conventionally in Burmese manuscripts as a pillar) and reaches (right) Tavatimsa. There he is shown seated on Sakka's stone throne (Pandukambalasilasana) under the *parijata* tree. The golden stupa is the Culamani shrine where Sakka placed the Bodhisatta's topknot. Below the Buddha, on either side of the cosmic axis on which are depicted its guardian creatures, are the lunar and solar symbols.

(c-d) The Buddha, now painted for the first time entirely gilded, descends the triple stairway with the gods in attendance. In some manuscripts, the three silver, gold and jewelled parts of the stairway are more clearly indicated, and sometimes Sariputta is shown kneeling at the foot of the stairway to welcome him back to earth.

The Buddha was absent in Tavatimsa for three months and during this period his followers became anxious to know where he was and when he would return. So Moggallana is said to have ascended into the Buddha's presence to inquire where he would reappear on earth. The Buddha chose the city of Sankassa where, in the Buddha's absence, Sariputta was preaching and answering people's questions on points of the Buddha's teachings. The occasion of the Buddha's descent is celebrated in Burma with a festival of lights on the full moon day of the month of Thadingyut (September/October) and marks the end of the Buddhist rainy season retreat.

## f.46-47 (p.58-59)
### The rainy seasons

(a) The Buddha's ninth rainy season at Kosambi. Among the kneeling monks are (left) some still with the conical hairstyle of hermits. These possibly represent the 500 hermits who were fed each year by three rich men who became the Buddha's disciples and each built a monastery for his use.

(b) The tenth rainy season in Parileyya forest where the Buddha went for solitude after discord at Kosambi among his followers. As well as the elephant who looked after the Buddha, a monkey is shown offering the Buddha a honeycomb. The monkey is not mentioned in the Burney or the full *Mala lingara* text, but appears in, for example, the *Dhammapada* commentary. The monkey and elephant are often depicted together in manuscript and other Burmese representations of this scene.

(c-d) The 11th and 12th rainy seasons, which the Buddha spent at a brahmin village (see the account of his preaching there below) and in a famine-stricken area where the generosity of some merchants ensured that the Buddha received food. White-robed and hatted brahmins are shown revering the Buddha and his monks, in front of whom are ranged offerings of food.

The rainy season (in Pali, *vassa*; in Burmese, *wa*) is a period of retreat for Buddhist monks who stay at their home monasteries and concentrate on study and meditation. The depiction of the Buddha's rainy seasons in most Burmese life of the Buddha manuscripts is quite monotonous, with the Buddha shown on successsive openings seated in simple

monastic structures. Omitted from this book are some further rainy seasons depicted in the Burney manuscripts which include the Buddha's conversion of a child-eating monster in Alavi and that of the murderer and robber Angulimala. Many well-loved sermons and rich imagery arise from the Buddha's years of ministry and retreats when he preached to and converted people from all walks of life. The 11th rainy season was spent in a village of brahmin farmers who at first criticized the Buddha as idle and refused him alms. The Buddha responded by stating that he too was a labourer, but one who ploughed and sowed to grow the fruit of salvation. Faith in the dhamma was, he explained, the seed he planted in men's hearts, austerity was the rain, wisdom the yoke, and mindfulness the ploughshare; truth was the hoe and effort was the ox that drew one to the deliverance from suffering that is Nibbana.

## OR. 14298
### f.3-4 (p.60-61)
### Sariputta's death

(a) Sariputta, lying on a bed with a red and white flowered covering, is visited by the gods and his aged mother (centre foreground).

(b-c) Sariputta's elaborate funeral pyre, decorated with the *karavika* bird (Burmese, *karaweik*) at the base of the catafalque and with prancing naga-dragons (*to-naya*) on a side panel. On the left rise the tiered roof spires and shrines erected in his honour by his mother and by Vissakamma, architect of the gods. His weeping mother kneels outside the enclosure while (left foreground) a crowd presses forward, trampling on Revati who had come to offer three golden flowers.

(d) Sariputta's relics are collected (foreground). Revati (upper) in a gilded heavenly pavilion descends in homage from Tavatimsa.

The Buddhist texts contain very little information on the Buddha's life from the 21st to the 44th rainy seasons (that is, from the age of 56 to 79), but to this period belongs the scheming of Devadatta against the Buddha. Among his attempts to kill the Buddha was his unleashing upon him of a fierce elephant, Nalagiri. The period leading up to the Buddha's 45th rainy season and the last ten months of his life are more closely chronicled. The Burney manuscripts omit many incidents from this period, and Or. 14298 opens with Sariputta's decision to return to his birthplace and to preach to his mother before his death. The northern Buddhist texts give the name of

Sariputta's village as Nalanda (which became a famous centre of Buddhist learning, with a great complex of temples and monasteries).

When Sariputta's relics were brought to him, the Buddha exhibited them to the monks as a powerful image of the truth that all is impermanent and subject to change. The Buddha delivered a long eulogy on Sariputta's qualities and directed that a stupa (in Pali, *thupa*; in Burmese, *zedi*) be erected to honour Sariputta's memory and pepetuate the remembrance of his virtues. On hearing the Buddha's words in honour of Sariputta, Ananda was moved to tears but the Buddha gently pointed out the futility of such grief. The Buddha's emphasis on impermanence should not be mistaken for pessimism, but as representing realism. His teachings offer followers joy and calm, and release from suffering.

## f.6-7 (p.62-63)
### Death of Moggallana and others

(a-d) The three funeral pyres depicted are, from left to right, Moggallana's, Rahula's and Kondanna's. Their deaths merit only a brief mention in the text, but the artist has delighted in a lavish, brightly-coloured portrayal of the coffins and catafalques. It is the custom in Burma for monks to have particularly elaborate funerals. The winged figures, half-human, half-bird (*kinnara* and, in the female form, *kinnari* – celestial creatures inhabiting the fabulous Himavanta or Himalayas) that support Kondanna's coffin often decorated the coffins of Burmese monks. The *kinnara* (Burmese, *kein-naya*) are said to have danced with joy at the Buddha's Enlightenment and they and other celestial creatures often feature as decorative motifs at monks' funerals. As befits such important disciples of the Buddha, the artist has provided them with most colourful and grand obsequies. Moggallana's violent death – he was beaten to death by robbers – was explained by the Buiddha as being the result of past bad deeds when in a previous existence he conspired to kill his parents. Rahula obtained Parinibbana after being reborn in Tavatimsa, while Kondanna spent his last 12 years in Himavanta, in the land of the mighty Chaddanta (tribe of elephants).

## f.9-10 (p.64-65)
### The final challenge by Mara

(a-b) The Buddha is visited by Mara (in white and gold robes). The large background flaming aureole of the Buddha is unusual.

(c-d) Ananda (upper) petitions the Buddha to use his powers and the Buddha (lower) preaches on the continuance of his dispensations.

This episode was Mara's last attempt to thwart the Buddha. The four bases of psychic powers (*iddhipada*) are concentration of will (*chanda*), of energy (*viriya*), of consciousness (*citta*) and of investigation (*vimamsa*) which enable one to reach the right path leading to the extinction of suffering. The Buddha cautioned against the improper use of such powers. On his final journey, he instructed that his disciples should pay great attention to 37 points of his teaching (*bodhi pakkhiya dhamma*) constituting true knowledge, divided into seven classes: the four subjects most deserving of attention (*cattaro satipatthana*); the four objects worthy of effort (*cattaro sammappadhana*); the four bases of psychic powers (*cattaro iddhipada*); the five necessary dispositions (*pancindriya*); the five resulting forces (*panca bala*); the seven requisites of enlightenment (*satta bojjhanga*); and the noble eightfold path (*ariya atthangika magga*).

## f.12-13 (p.66-67)
### The last meal

(a) The Buddha preaches on the four great authorities.

(b) The Buddha, seated in a mango grove, is invited by Cunda to a meal.

(c-d) The Buddha, seated with his monks on the monastery verandah within a curtained enclosure, is served his last meal. The red lacquer covered containers are decorated with gilded flowers.

(d, upper) A man, standing, digs a hole to bury the remains of the Buddha's food, as directed by the Buddha.

The four great authorities (*mahapadesa*) or points of citation and reference are the means by which the words of the Buddha are tested, his actual doctrine determined and clarified.

There is some uncertainty over what the last meal consisted of, although the Burmese texts always refer to it as a pork dish. The Pali term is *sukaramaddava* which has been variously interpreted as sweetened pork, or a kind of mushroom, or some specially flavoured dish.

## f.14-15 (p.68-69)
### The last journey

(a-b) A team of ox carts (right) links this scene with the next. Ananda (b, foreground) fills the Buddha's bowl with water from the stream (painted here without the stylized hoops of the other Burney manuscript) and (upper left) presents it to the Buddha.

(c-d) The Malla prince (upper right) presents two robes to the Buddha and Ananda (d, lower) in turn presents his to the Buddha.

Prince Pukkusa had been a disciple of the sage Alara and told how once when Alara was resting 500 ox carts had passed him by without his noticing. To this the Buddha responded by telling Pukkusa of how he had demonstrated even greater calmness of mind during a particularly violent storm. Pukkusa thereupon took refuge in the three jewels, and became a devoted lay supporter of the Buddha. When Pukkusa presented two robes of golden cloth to the Buddha, the Buddha instructed him to offer one to Ananda, both as a mark of favour to Ananda for his 25 years of stewardship and so that Pukkusa would accrue even greater merit by making a gift both to the Buddha and to the order of monks in the person of Ananda.

## f.16-17 (p.70-71)
### The Buddha rests

(a-b) The Buddha bathes (upper left) and then rests on his right side in a curtained enclosure. Standing to the left of the tree and folding a robe for the Buddha to lie on is the monk Cunda.

(c-d) The musicians and dancers (foreground) under a domed structure link this scene to the next which depicts the Buddha's death and obsequies. The instruments are much as depicted in an earlier scene of a Burmese orchestra (see p.27-28), but with the addition of bamboo clappers (*wa let-bkot*). The figure of the Buddha with four kneeling monks (c, upper) probably represents his preaching along the way to Kusinara, or his last admonitions to the monks.

The monk Cunda who was with the Buddha on his last journey was a disciple of some eminence and is not to be confused with the Cunda who gave the Buddha his last meal. Some texts maintain that he was Sariputta's younger brother. The Burney manuscript omits the story of the Buddha's last convert Subhadda, who came to see the Buddha on his last night. Although Ananda did not wish to admit Subhadda to the Buddha's presence, the Buddha insisted on seeing him and he was received into the monkhood.

## f.18-19 (p.72-73)
### The Buddha attains Parinibbana

(a-b) The Buddha lies on a couch (with a canopy) on his right side, with his head to the north and his feet one upon the other. In front of him are Ananda and another grieving monk (Cunda?) and gods, brahmins and lay men and women. The lady (b, centre) in royal white and gold robes and headdress, must represent one of the Malla queens – as the texts state that in the first watch of the night the Malla royalty came to pay their respects.

(c-d) The funeral procession with white and gilded umbrellas held above the bier. Mallika kneels (c, foreground) after presenting a golden shroud.

(d, upper) Kassapa and other monks are shown on their way to Kusinara; unusually, some lines of explanatory Burmese text are written above this scene.

Between Pava and the sala grove at Kusinara the Buddha, in his weakened state, had to make 25 stops to rest. Ananda queried the Buddha's choice of insignificant Kusinara to die in and it is said that the Buddha made the effort to reach Kusinara for several reasons: in order to preach on its former glory (the *Mahasudassana sutta*), to be able to convert Subhadda, and so that the brahmin Dona could distribute his relics. The Buddha's last words were reported to be: '*Vayadhamma samkhara, appamadena sampadetha*' – sometimes (mis)rendered as 'Work out your salvation with diligence'.

## f.20-21 (p.74-75)
### The cremation

(a-b) Kassapa (foreground) kneels before the Buddha's coffin from which protrude his gilded feet. Celestial half-human, half-bird figures support the corners of the catafalque (just as on Kondanna's and monks' coffins in old Burma). In a continuation of the scene from the previous opening, Kassapa (a, upper left) meets a naked ascetic carrying the fabulous *mandarava* flower.

(c-d) The Malla princes pour water from golden urns, while water springs in a cascade from the sala trees.

The scornful remarks of the monk Subhadda (not the same as the Buddha's last convert) who was formerly a barber and bore the Buddha a grudge, caused Kassapa to resolve to hold a general council of monks to ascertain correctly the Buddha's teachings. This was held at Rajagaha soon after the Buddha's death. The second council was held a century later at Vesali and the third at Pataliputta (Patna) in the third century BC under the patronage of the Emperor Asoka. The number of Buddhist Councils (and their locations) accepted as authentic varies from country to country, with Thailand acknowledging as many as ten, but Sri Lanka and Burma only six. The fourth council (at which the texts were committed to writing) was held in the last century BC in Sri Lanka, and the fifth, according to Burmese tradition, at Mandalay in 1871 (but according to Sinhalese tradition in 1865 at Ratanapura in Sri Lanka), and the sixth at Rangoon in 1954-56.

## f.22-23 (p.76-77)
### Obsequies

(a-c) The Buddha's relics, in a golden urn, are carried in procession on elephantback, along a road fenced by latticework. The attendants all wear white, the colour of mourning.

(d) The relics are guarded in a tiered pavilion.

## f.24-25 (p.78-79)
### Distribution of the relics

(a) The brahmin Dona, standing in front of the urn, begins the distribution of the relics. In the sky, Sakka carries off the relic which Dona had secreted (some manuscripts show Sakka plucking the relic from Dona's headdress where he had hidden it).

According to some accounts, the Naga, shown at Dona's feet, received a tooth relic (or was entrusted with it by the Koliyas) which was enshrined in the Naga world. The monk hovering in the air (to the right of Sakka) is Kassapa who, after the main relics were distributed to the claimants and enshrined in separate places, became anxious and collected them together and buried them in Rajagaha for Asoka, the great Indian ruler converted to Buddhism, to discover in the future.

(b-d) The white-robed, gold crowned kings, together with royal attendants, are shown kneeling in line (foreground) to receive the relics and (above) bearing them away, white umbrellas now unfurled and held aloft, for enshrinement in their kingdoms.

The relics were claimed by the Malla kings/princes of Kusinara and of Pava, by King Ajatasattu of Magadha, by the Licchavis of Vesali, the Sakyas of Kapilavatthu, the Bulis of Allakappa, the Koliyas of Ramagama and the brahmin chief of Vethadipa. The Moriyas of Pipphalivana made a late claim and were given the embers of the funeral pyre, while Dona kept the golden vessel to enshrine. Buddhist tradition states that Kassapa safeguarded the relics by having them enshrined together in Rajagaha, and that Emperor Asoka rediscovered the sacred relics and distributed them far and wide, building 84,000 stupa reliquaries.

The funeral procession of the Buddha.
Or. 14298, f. 19, detail.

# Glossary

The main Pali names in the picture text are given with diacritics, followed in brackets by their Burmese form of pronunciation where differing substantially.

Ajapāla-nigrodha – goatherds' banyan tree

Ajātasattu – successor to and son of King Bimbisāra

Āḷāra – one of the Bodhisatta's first teachers

Ānanda – the Buddha's disciple and steward

Animisa – 'unblinking'; the second station of the Buddha

Anomā – river crossed by the Bodhisatta on his departure

Anotatta – one of seven great lakes in Buddhist cosmology

Anupiya – township and mango grove

Aparajita – 'unconquered' throne of the Buddha

Asoka – great Buddhist ruler, ca. 269-231 BC

Assaji – the fifth of the Pañcavaggiyā monks

Bhallika – younger merchant brother

Bhāradvāja – a brahmin farming clan

Bimbisāra (Beimbathaya) – king of Magadha

Bodhisatta (Bawdithat) – the Buddha-to-be (known as *Hpaya-laung* in Burmese)

Brahmā (Byamma) – a class of higher gods

Cāpāla-cetiya – a shrine near Vesāli

Channa (Hsanna) – Gotama's attendant/charioteer

Cūḷāmaṇi (Sulamani) – shrine in Tāvatiṃsa heaven

Cunda (Sonda) – (a) a monk (2) a goldsmith's son

Dakkhiṇāgiri – district to south of Rājagaha

Devadaha – township of the Sakyans

Dīpaṅkara – a Buddha

Doṇa – brahmin who divided the relics

Ekanāla – a brahmin village

Ghaṭīkāra – one of the great Brahmas

Ghositārāma – a monastery

Girimekhala – Mara's war elephant

Gotama – personal name of the Buddha

Hiraññavatī – river near which the Buddha died

Huhuṅkajātika – a brahmin, named onamatopoeically (from his humming and hawing)

Isipatana – place where the Buddha preached his first sermon

Jambudīpa (Zabu-deik-kyun or Zabu-dipa) – 'rose-apple' island

Jetavana (Zetawun) – a monastery and park in Sāvatthi

Jetuttara – capital city of King Sañjaya

Jūjaka (Zuzaka) – a brahmin to whom Prince Vessantara gave his children

Kakutthā – river in which the Buddha bathed on his last journey

Kāla – see Mahākāla

Kāḷadevala – a brahmin sage; also known as Asita

Kanthaka – Prince Siddhattha's horse

Kapilavatthu (Kapilawut) – capital of the Sakyas, the Buddha's clan

Kassapa – see Uruvela-Kassapa

Kisāgotami – a maiden/princess of Kapilavatthu

Kolita – Moggallāna's former name

Koṇḍañña (Kundinya) – youngest of the soothsayers and one of the first five disciples; also known as Aññāta-Koṇḍañña

Kosambī (Kawthambi) – a city

Kusinārā – village where the Buddha died

Lumbinī – a park, grove of sāla trees, where the Buddha was born

Magadha – kingdom, ruled by Bimbisāra

Mahākāla – a Nāga (serpent) king; also known as Kāḷanāga

Mahāmāyā – the Buddha's mother ('great Māyā')

Malla (Manla) – a people and their country

Mallikā – lady who gives shroud at funeral procession

Mandārava – fabulous flower

Māra (Man Nat) – the Evil One

Māyā – see Mahāmāyā

Meru, Mount (Myin-mo) – the central cosmic mountain axis; also known as Sineru or Sumeru

Moggallāna (Maukgalan) – one of the Buddha's chief disciples

Mucalinda – a Nāga king; also name of the tree and lake associated with him

Nālaka – Sāriputta's birthplace

Nerañjara – a river

Pañcavaggiyā (Pyinsa weggi) – five ascetics who became the Buddha's first disciples

Paṇḍava – hill near Rājagaha

Paṇḍukambalasilāsana – great stone throne of Sakka

Pārijāta (or Pāricchattaka) – coral tree in Tāvatimsa

Pārileyya (or Pārileyyaka) – township near Kosambī

Pāvā – city where the Buddha received his last meal

Pukkusa – a Malla prince

Rāhula – son of Gotama Buddha

Rājagaha (Yazagyo) – capital of Magadha

Rājayatana – tree (called *lin-lun* in Burmese)

Revatī – Sāriputta's former nurse

Sahampati – a great Brahma

Sakka (Thagya-min) – a god, king of Tāvatimsa

Sāla (or sal) – trees (*shorea robusta* ; called *in-gyin* in Burmese) associated with Buddha's birth and death

Sañjaya – (1) father of Prince Vessantara (2) first teacher of Sāriputta and Moggallāna

Sankassa – a city, where the Buddha descended from heaven

Sāriputta (Tharipoktara) – one of the Buddha's chief disciples

Sāvatthi – capital of Kosala

Senānī – father of Sujātā

Setaketu – Gotama's name while in Tusita heaven

Siddhattha (Theikdat min-tha) – Gotama Buddha's name as a prince

Sivirattha – kingdom of King Sañjaya

Sotthiya – a grass-cutter

Subhadda – (1) a dissident monk (2) the Buddha's last convert

Suddhodana – king of Kapilavatthu and father of Gotama Buddha

Sujātā (Thuzata) – lady who gave milk-rice to the Bodhisatta

Sumedha (Thumeda) – the Bodhisatta in the time of Dīpankara Buddha

Sumsumāragiri – a city in Bhaggā country

Suppabuddha – the Bodhisatta's father-in-law

Tapussa – elder merchant brother

Tāvatimsa (Tawadeintha-bon) – heaven of the 33 gods

Tusita (Tuthita-bon) – heaven of the 'blissful'

Uddaka – one of the Bodhisatta's first teachers

Ukkalā (or Ukkalāpa) – home city of the merchant brothers

Upaka – an ascetic who met the Buddha on his way to the deer park

Upatissa – Sāriputta's former name

Uruvelā – township of the Mallas

Uruvelā-Kassapa – eldest of the three hermit brothers converted by the Buddha

Vankagiri – a mountain, place of Prince Vessantara's banishment

Veluvana (Weluwun) – bamboo grove donated by King Bimbisāra

Verañjā – a town where the Buddha spent the 12th rainy season

Vesāli (Wethali) – capital city of the Licchavī

Vessantara (Wethandaya min-tha) – the Bodhisatta's name in his penultimate human rebirth

Yasa (Yatha) – rich man's son; the Buddha's first lay convert

Yasodharā (Yathawdaya) – wife of Prince Siddhattha

Yugandhara – first mountain range surrounding the cosmic axis

The monkey and elephant of Parileyya forest (the Buddha's tenth rainy season). Or. 14297, f. 46, detail.

95

© 1993 The British Library Board
First published 1993 by The British Library, Great
Russell Street, London WC1B 3DG

Published in North and South America
by Pomegranate Artbooks, Petaluma, California 94975

British Library Cataloguing in Publication Data
Herbert, Patricia M.
  The Life of the Buddha
  1. Buddha
  I. Title
  294.363
  ISBN 0 7123 0188 7

Designed by Roger Davies
Set in Garamond on Ventura
Printed by Jolly and Barber, UK